IT'S GRIMMY

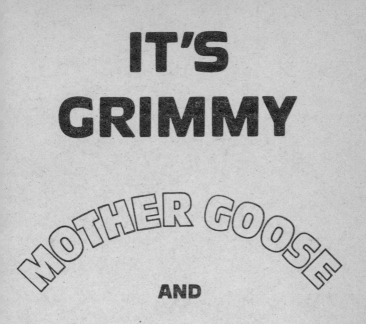

MOTHER GOOSE

AND

TOR

A TOM DOHERTY ASSOCIATES BOOK
NEW YORK

MOTHER GOOSE AND GRIMM: IT'S GRIMMY

TM and Copyright © 1990 Grimmy, Inc. Licensed by MGM/UA.

A TOR Book
Published by Tom Doherty Associates, Inc.
49 West 24 Street
New York, NY 10010

ISBN: 0-812-50568-9   Can. ISBN: 0-812-50569-7

First Tor edition: February 1990

Printed in the United States of America

0 9 8 7 6 5 4 3 2 1

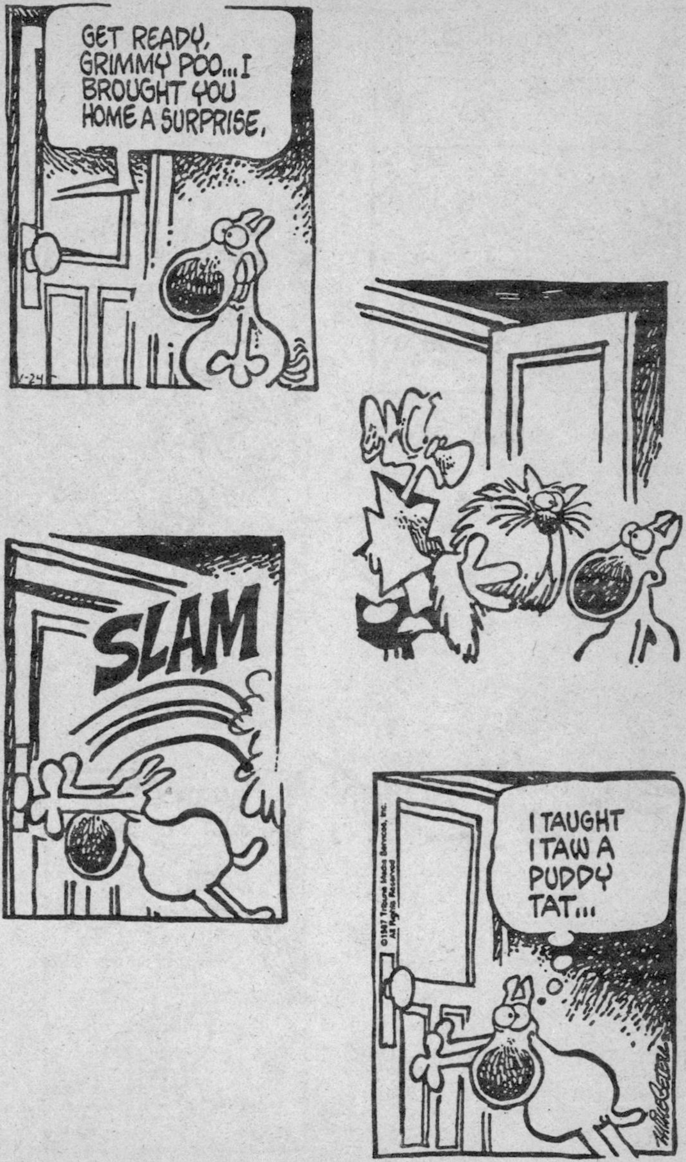
GET READY, GRIMMY POO...I BROUGHT YOU HOME A SURPRISE.
SLAM
I TAUGHT I TAW A PUDDY TAT...
©1987 Tribune Media Services, Inc.
All Rights Reserved

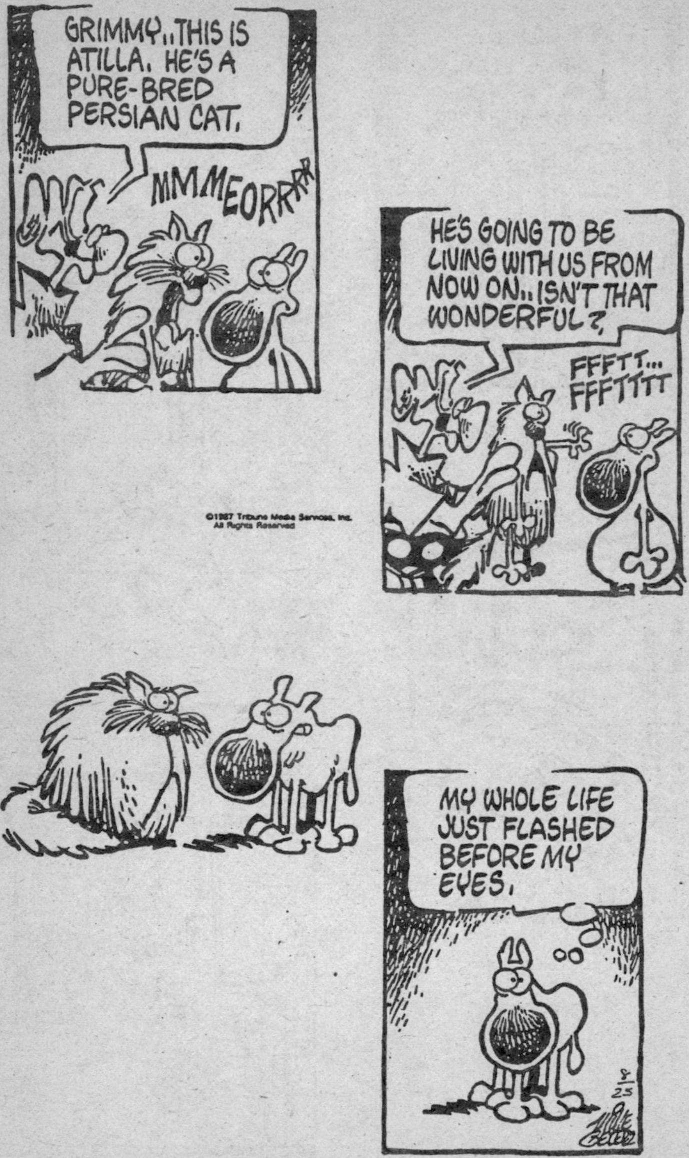
GRIMMY.. THIS IS ATILLA. HE'S A PURE-BRED PERSIAN CAT.
MMMEORRRRR
HE'S GOING TO BE LIVING WITH US FROM NOW ON.. ISN'T THAT WONDERFUL?
FFFTT... FFFTTTT
MY WHOLE LIFE JUST FLASHED BEFORE MY EYES.
8/25

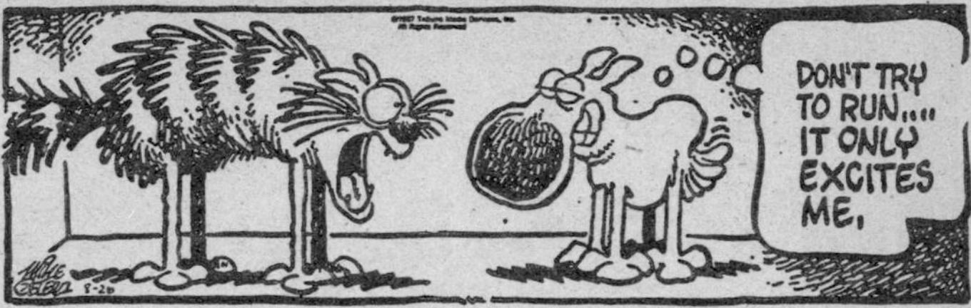
DON'T TRY TO RUN.... IT ONLY EXCITES ME.

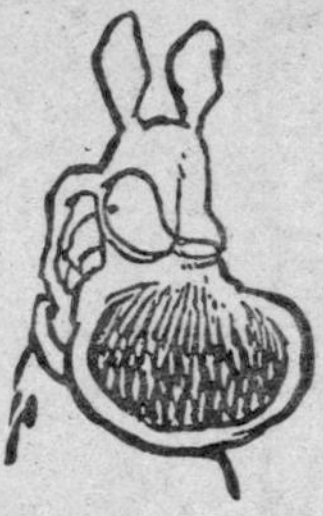

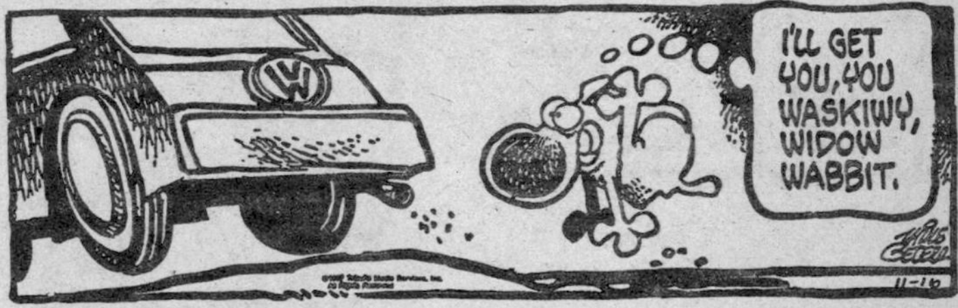
I'LL GET YOU, YOU WASKIWY, WIDOW WABBIT.

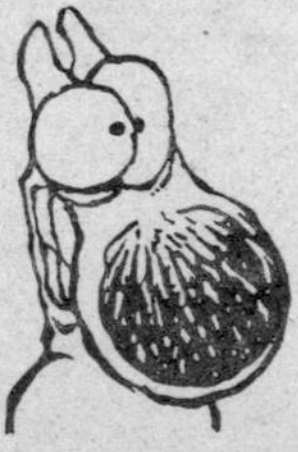

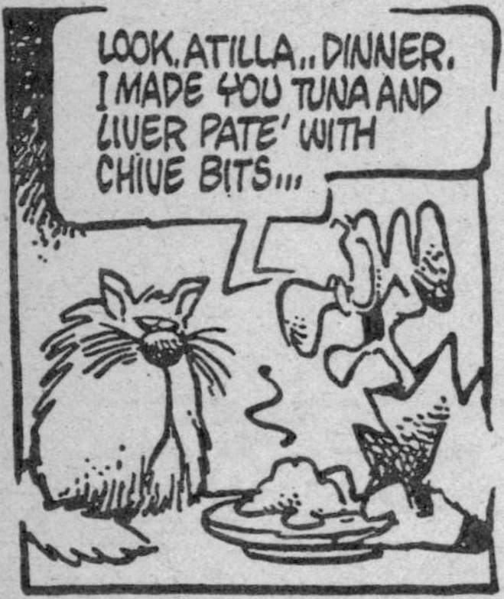
LOOK, ATILLA.. DINNER. I MADE YOU TUNA AND LIVER PATE' WITH CHIVE BITS...

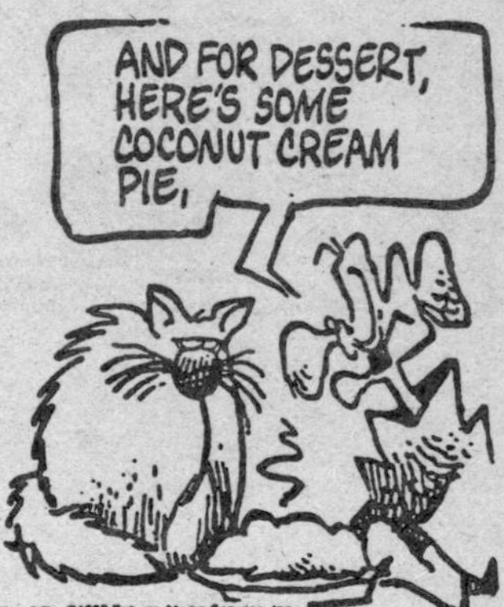
AND FOR DESSERT, HERE'S SOME COCONUT CREAM PIE,

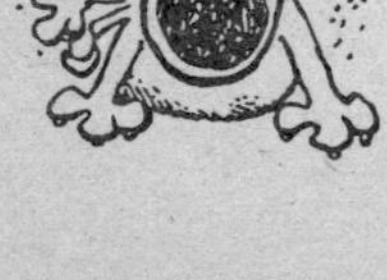

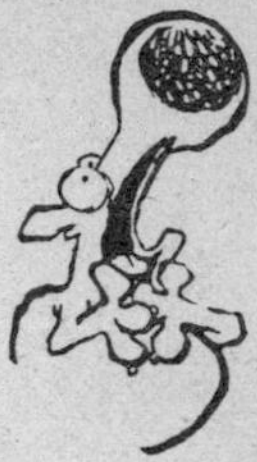

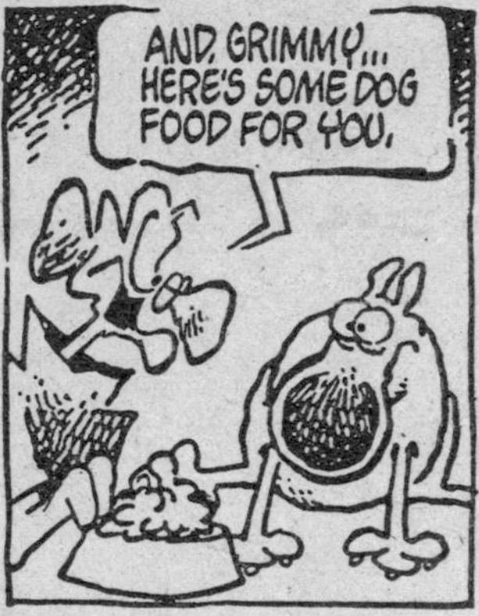
AND, GRIMMY...
HERE'S SOME DOG
FOOD FOR YOU.

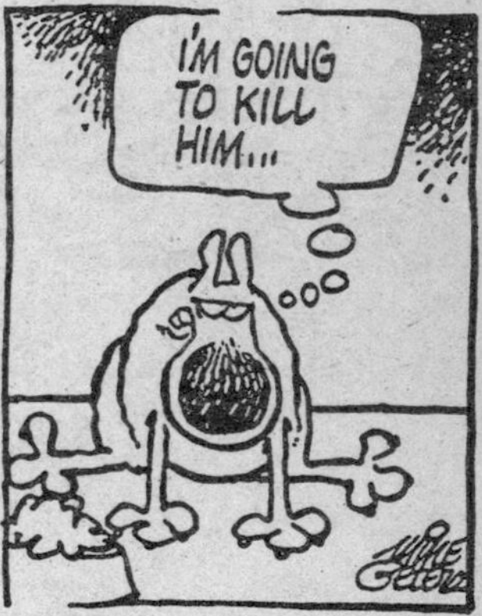
I'M GOING
TO KILL
HIM...

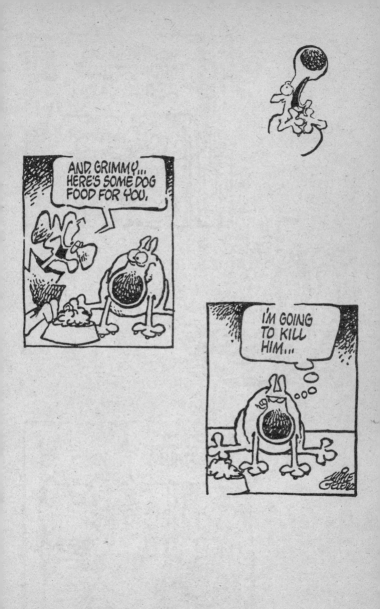

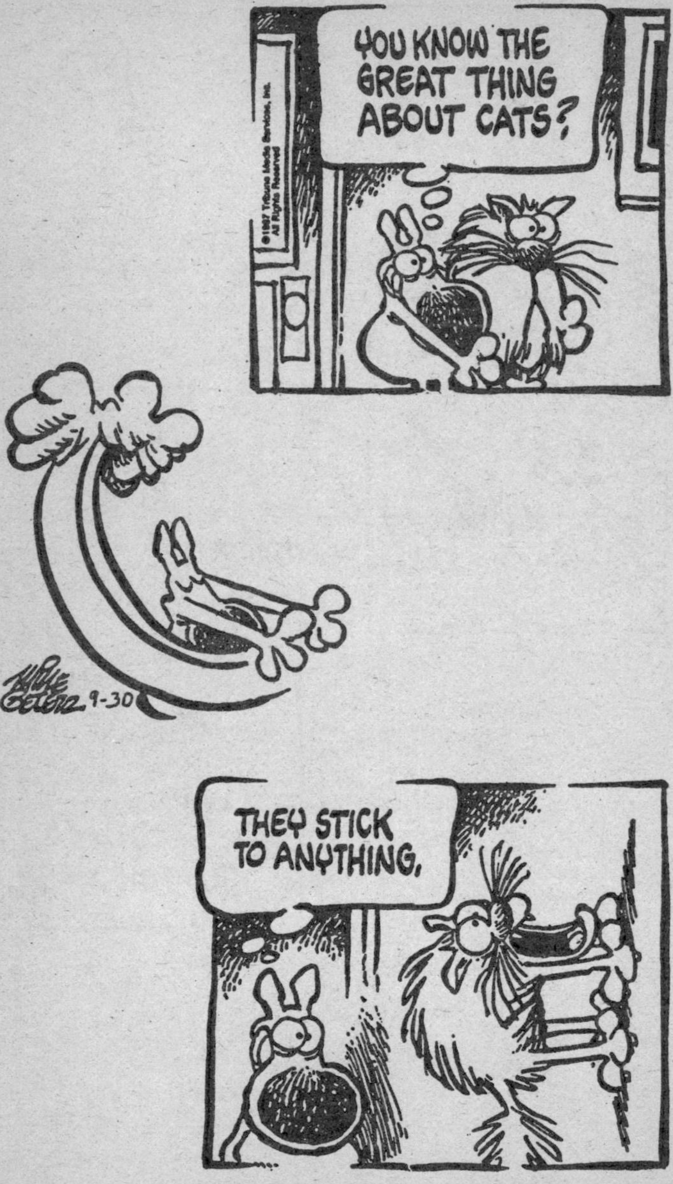
YOU KNOW THE GREAT THING ABOUT CATS?
©1997 Tribune Media Services, Inc. All Rights Reserved
THEY STICK TO ANYTHING.
9-30

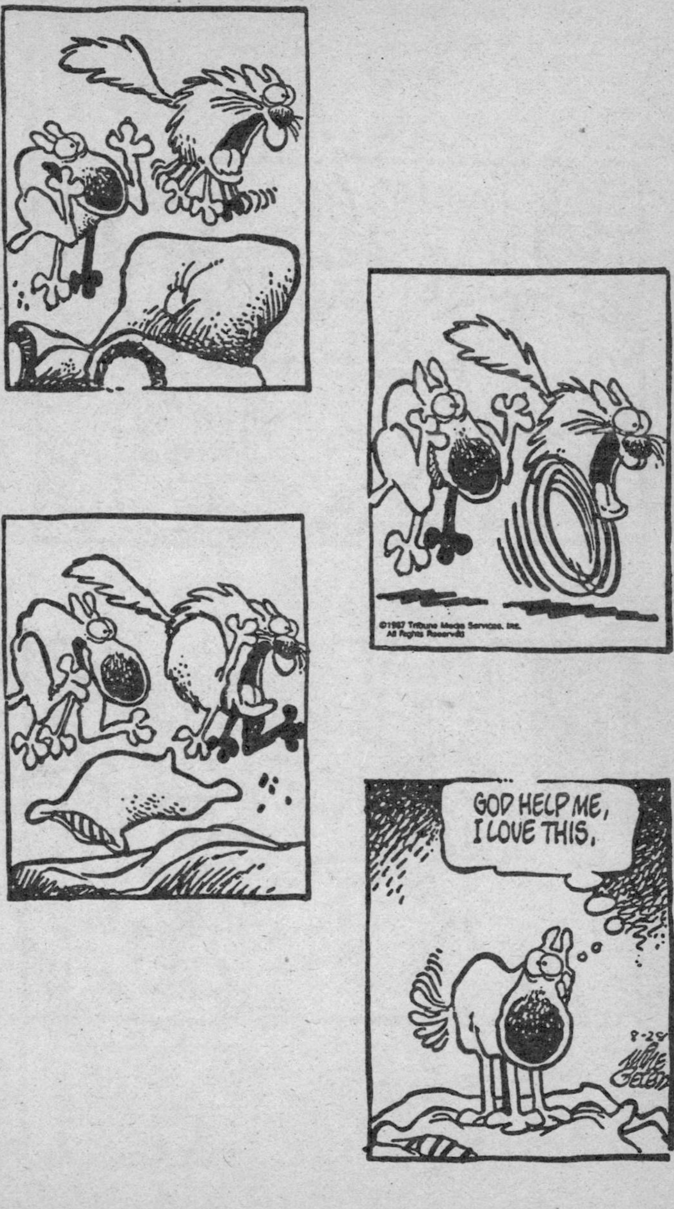
©1987 Tribune Media Services, Inc.
All Rights Reserved
GOD HELP ME,
I LOVE THIS.
8-28

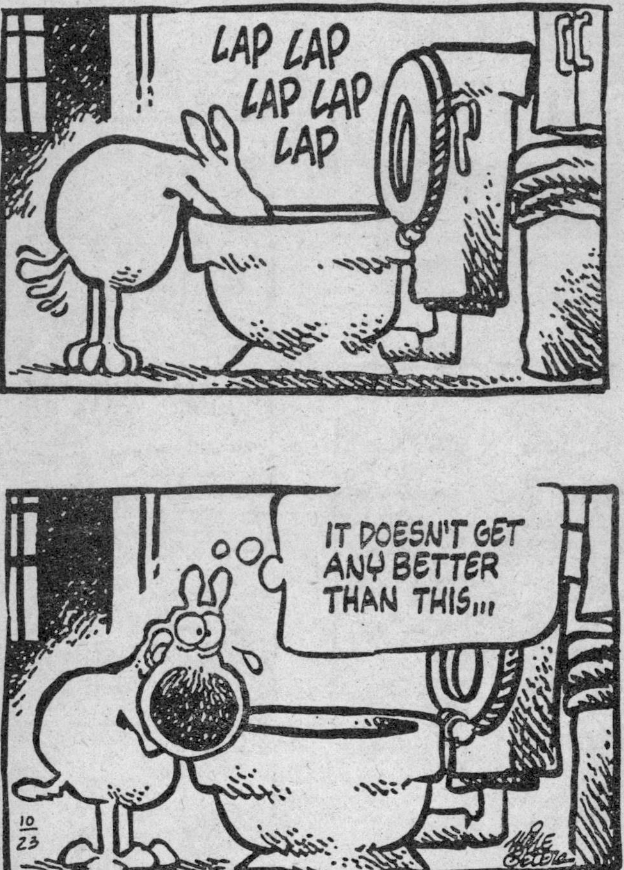
LAP LAP
LAP LAP
LAP
IT DOESN'T GET ANY BETTER THAN THIS,,,
10/23

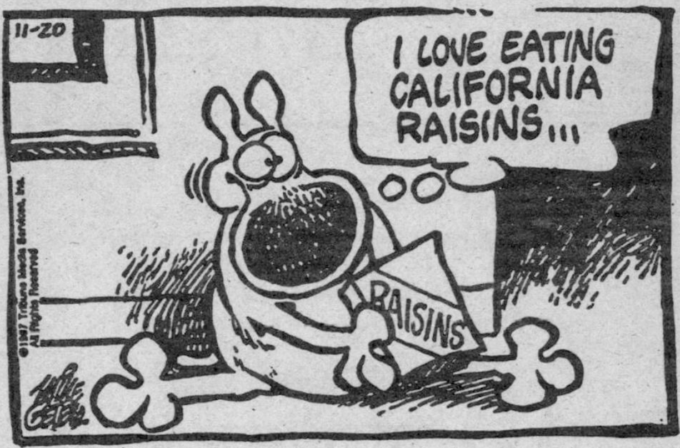
11-20
I LOVE EATING CALIFORNIA RAISINS...
RAISINS
©1987 Tribune Media Services, Inc. All Rights Reserved

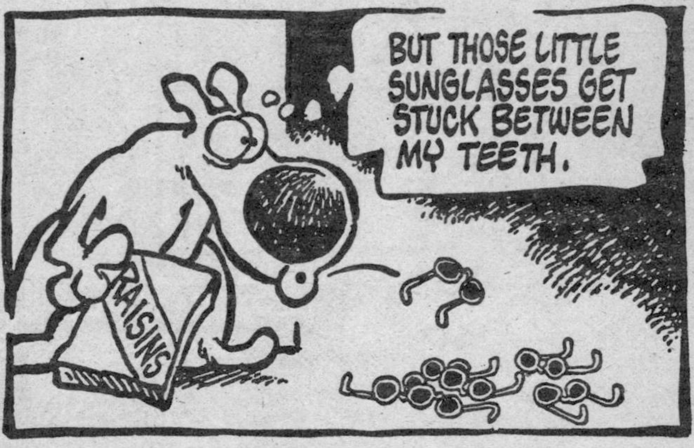
BUT THOSE LITTLE SUNGLASSES GET STUCK BETWEEN MY TEETH.
RAISINS

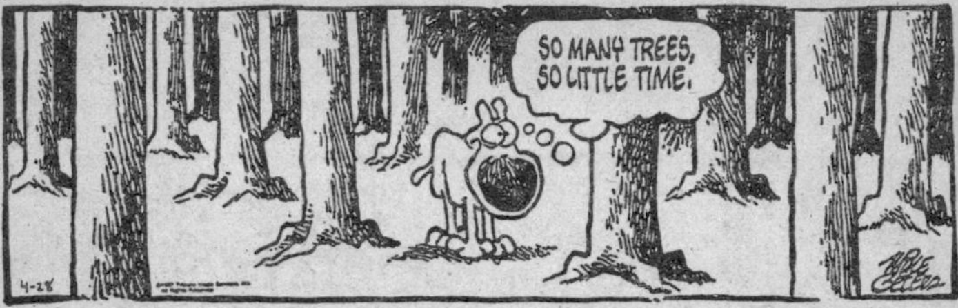
SO MANY TREES, SO LITTLE TIME.
4-28

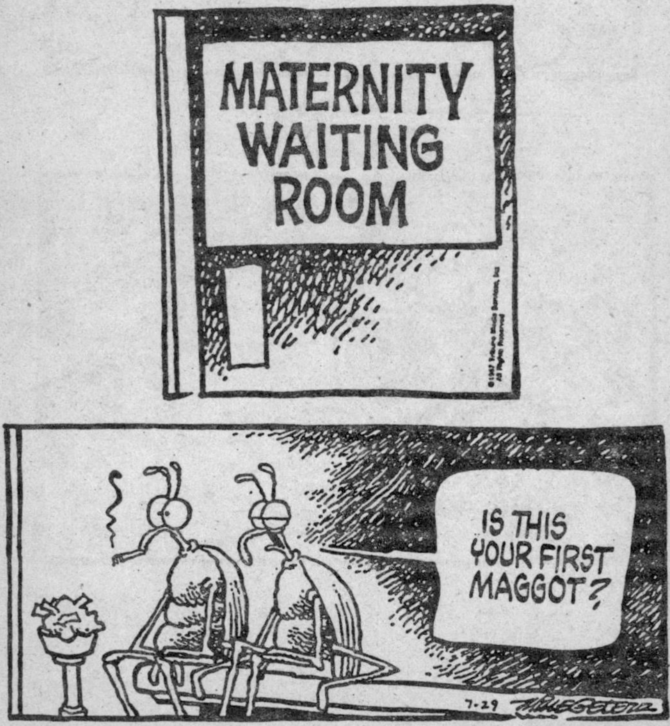
MATERNITY WAITING ROOM
IS THIS YOUR FIRST MAGGOT?
7-29

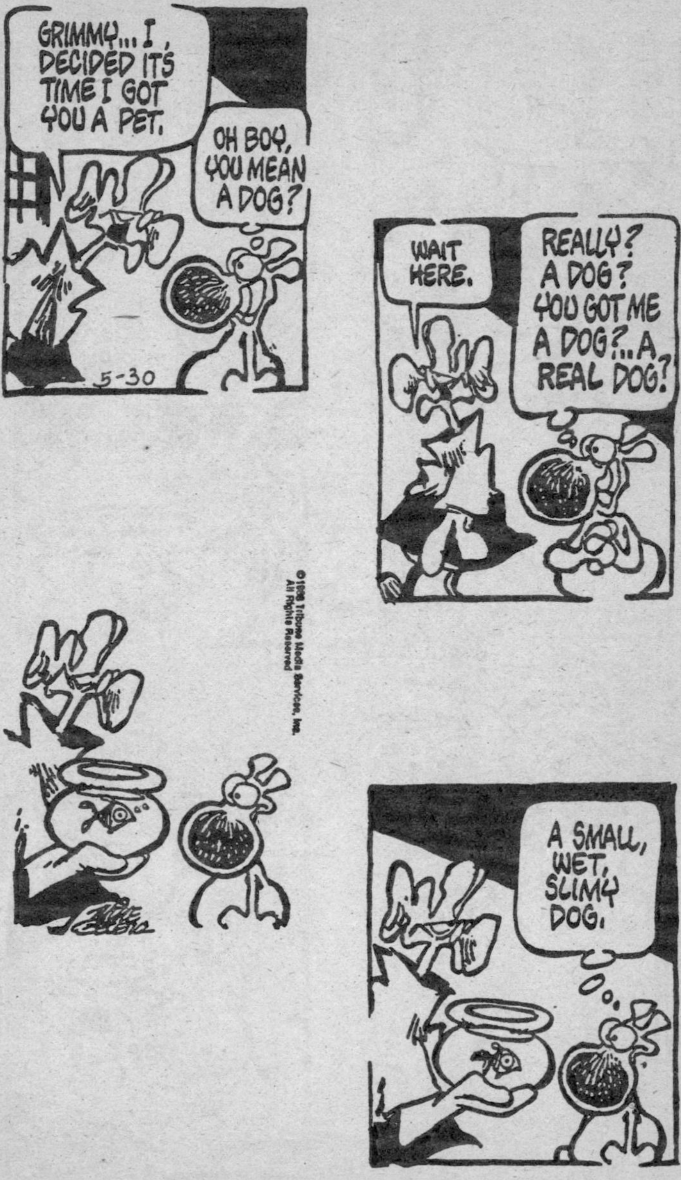
GRIMMY... I, DECIDED IT'S TIME I GOT YOU A PET.
OH BOY, YOU MEAN A DOG?
5-30
WAIT HERE.
REALLY? A DOG? YOU GOT ME A DOG?...A REAL DOG?
A SMALL, WET, SLIMY DOG.
Tribune Media Services, Inc.
All Rights Reserved

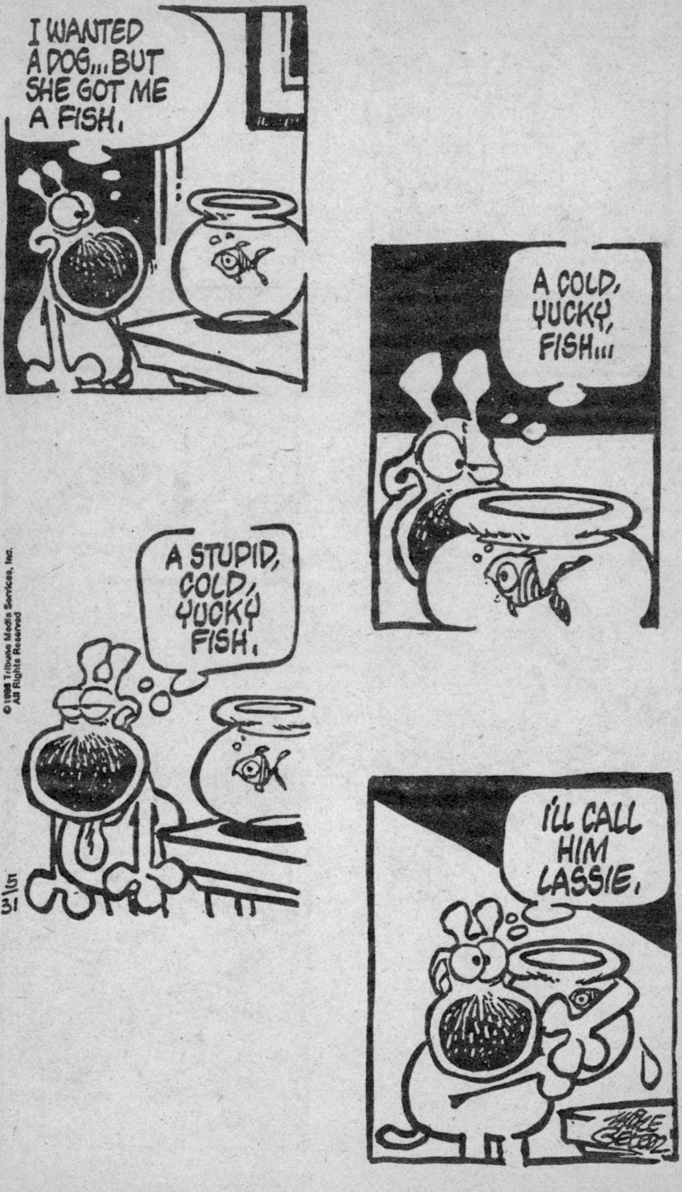
I WANTED A DOG... BUT SHE GOT ME A FISH.
A COLD, YUCKY, FISH...
A STUPID, COLD, YUCKY FISH.
I'LL CALL HIM LASSIE.

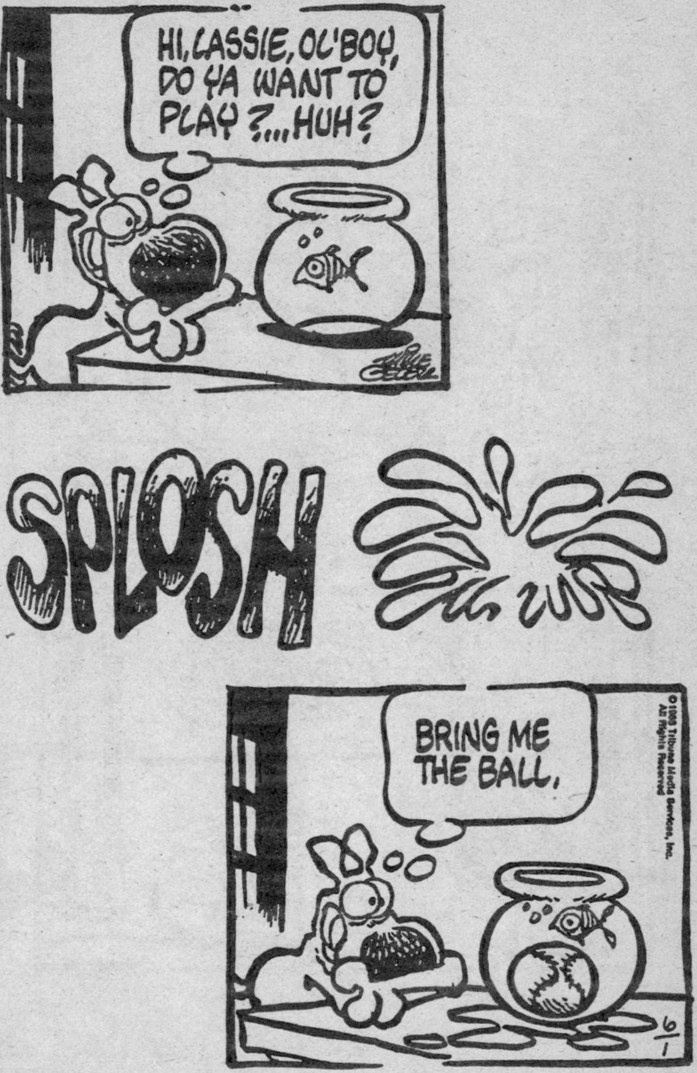
HI, LASSIE, OL'BOY, DO YA WANT TO PLAY ?... HUH?
SPLOSH
BRING ME THE BALL.
6/1

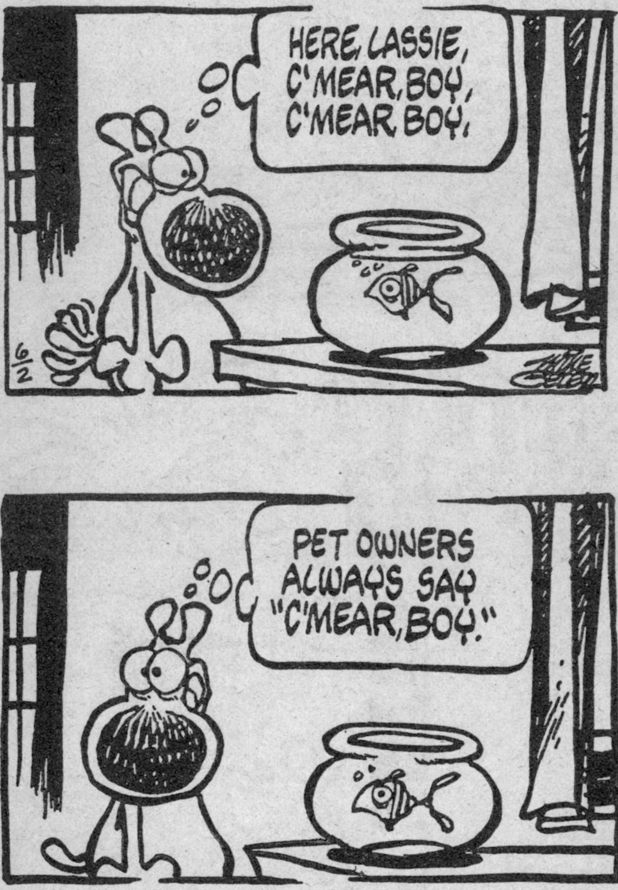
HERE, LASSIE, C'MEAR, BOY, C'MEAR, BOY.
6/2
PET OWNERS ALWAYS SAY "C'MEAR, BOY."

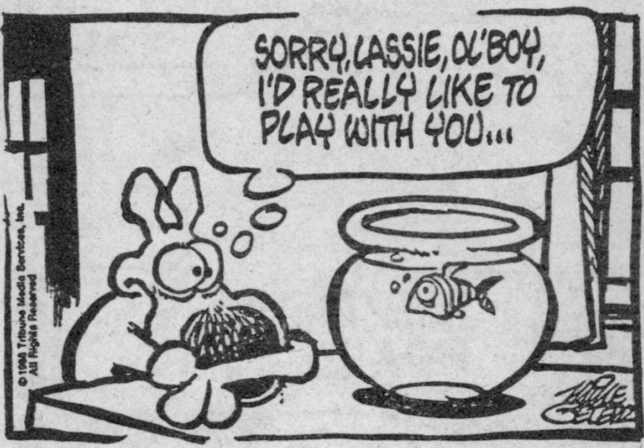
SORRY, LASSIE, OL'BOY, I'D REALLY LIKE TO PLAY WITH YOU...
© 1988 Tribune Media Services, Inc.
All Rights Reserved

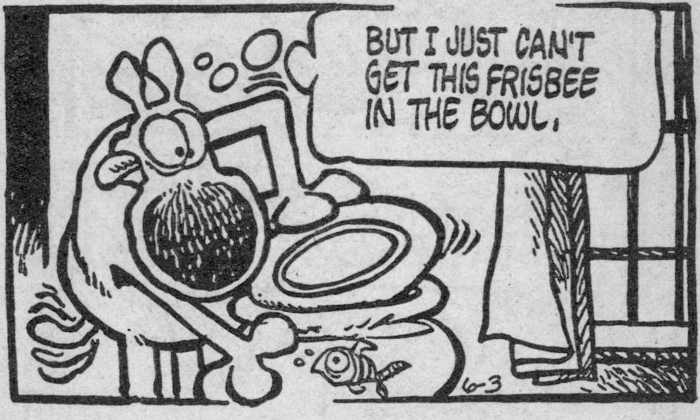
BUT I JUST CAN'T GET THIS FRISBEE IN THE BOWL.
6-3

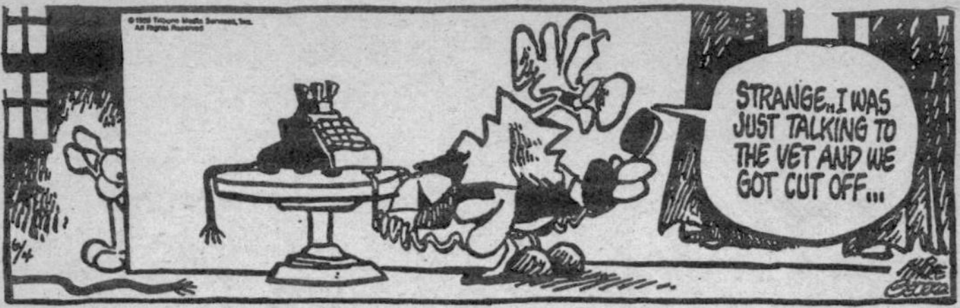
STRANGE..I WAS JUST TALKING TO THE VET AND WE GOT CUT OFF...

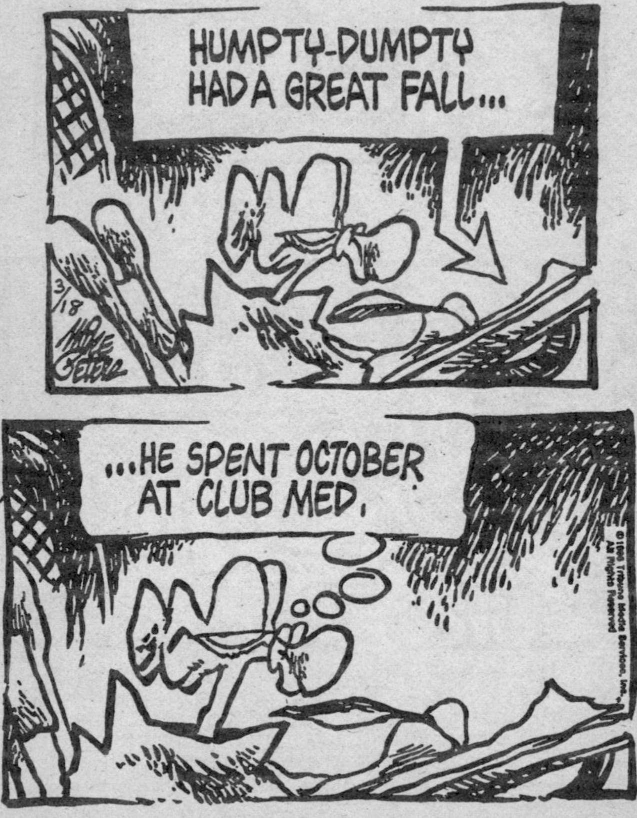
HUMPTY-DUMPTY HAD A GREAT FALL...
...HE SPENT OCTOBER AT CLUB MED.

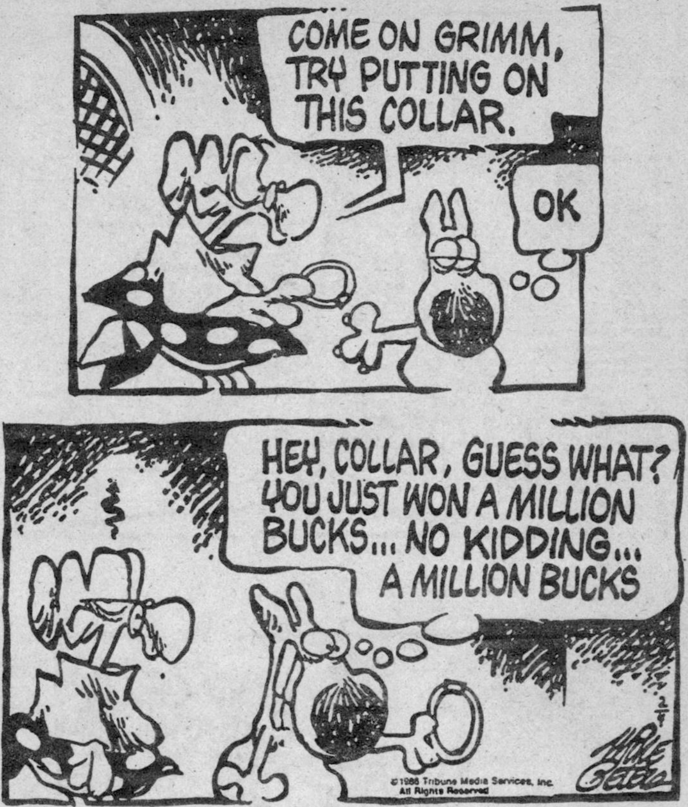
COME ON GRIMM, TRY PUTTING ON THIS COLLAR.
OK
HEY, COLLAR, GUESS WHAT? YOU JUST WON A MILLION BUCKS... NO KIDDING... A MILLION BUCKS
©1988 Tribune Media Services, Inc. All Rights Reserved

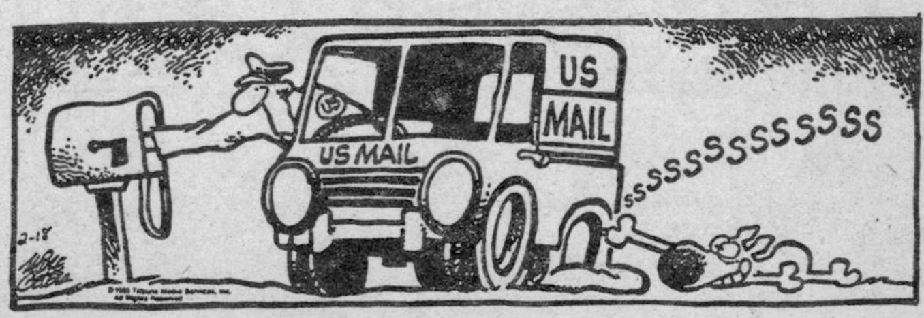
US MAIL
US MAIL
sSSSSSSSSSSSSSS
2-18

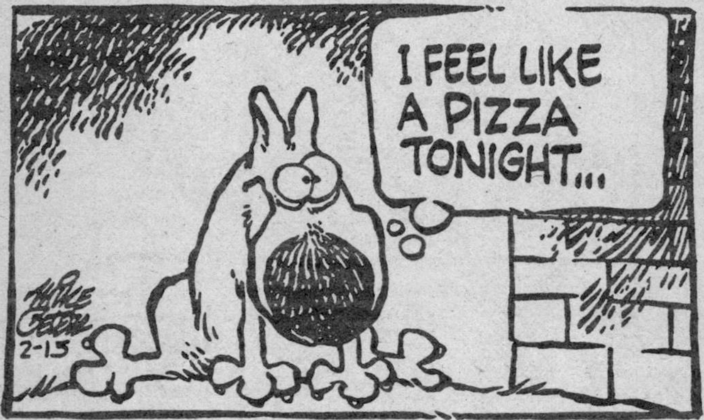
I FEEL LIKE A PIZZA TONIGHT...

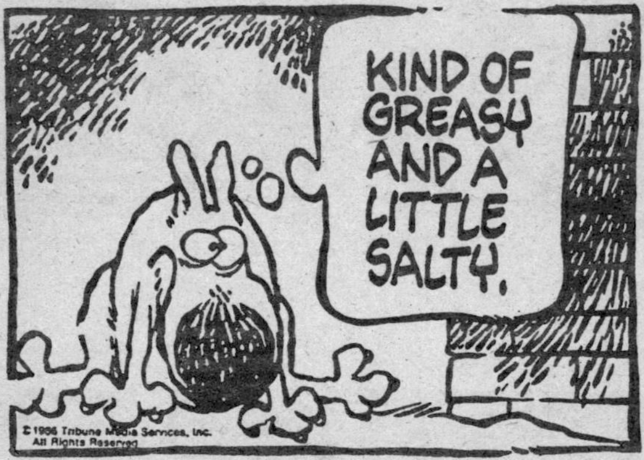
KIND OF GREASY AND A LITTLE SALTY.
©1986 Tribune Media Services, Inc. All Rights Reserved

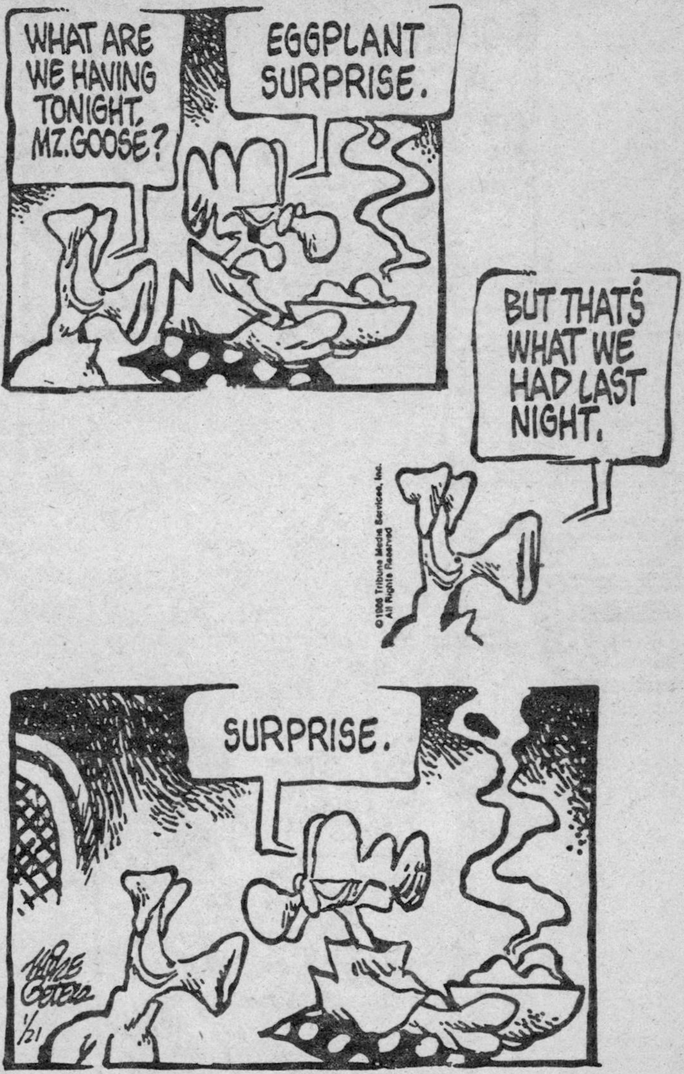

WHAT ARE WE HAVING TONIGHT, MZ.GOOSE?
EGGPLANT SURPRISE.
BUT THAT'S WHAT WE HAD LAST NIGHT.
SURPRISE.
©1986 Tribune Media Services, Inc.
All Rights Reserved
MIKE PETERS
1/21

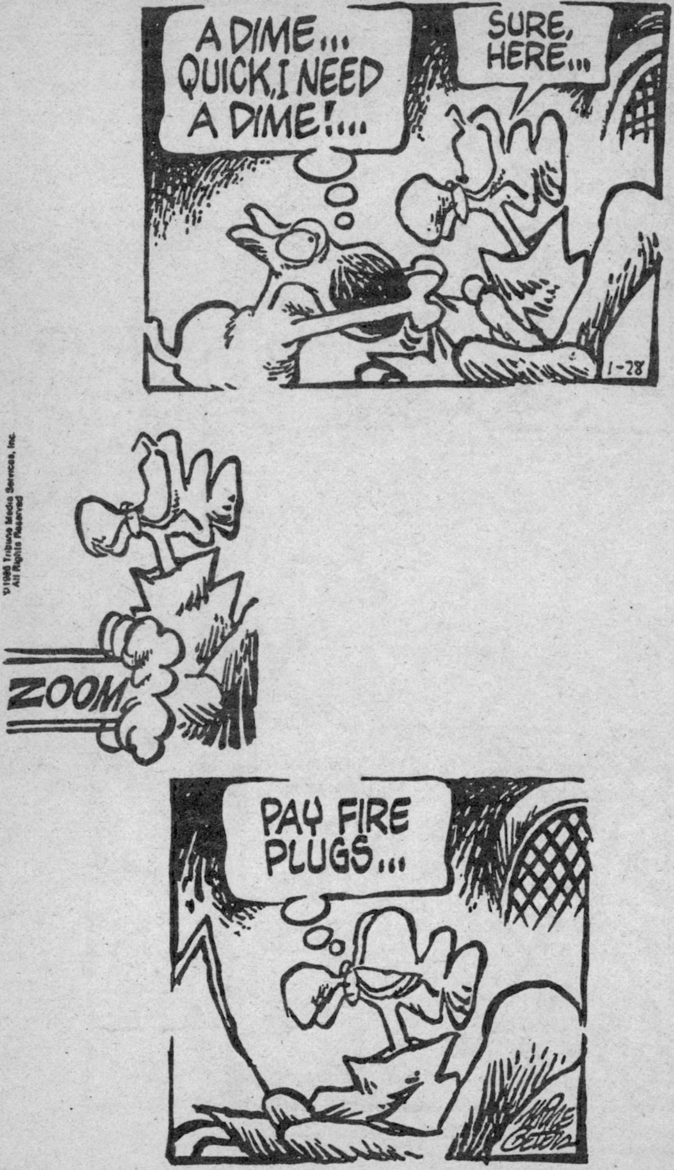
A DIME... QUICK, I NEED A DIME!...
SURE, HERE...
1-28
ZOOM
PAY FIRE PLUGS...
Tribune Media Services, Inc.
All Rights Reserved

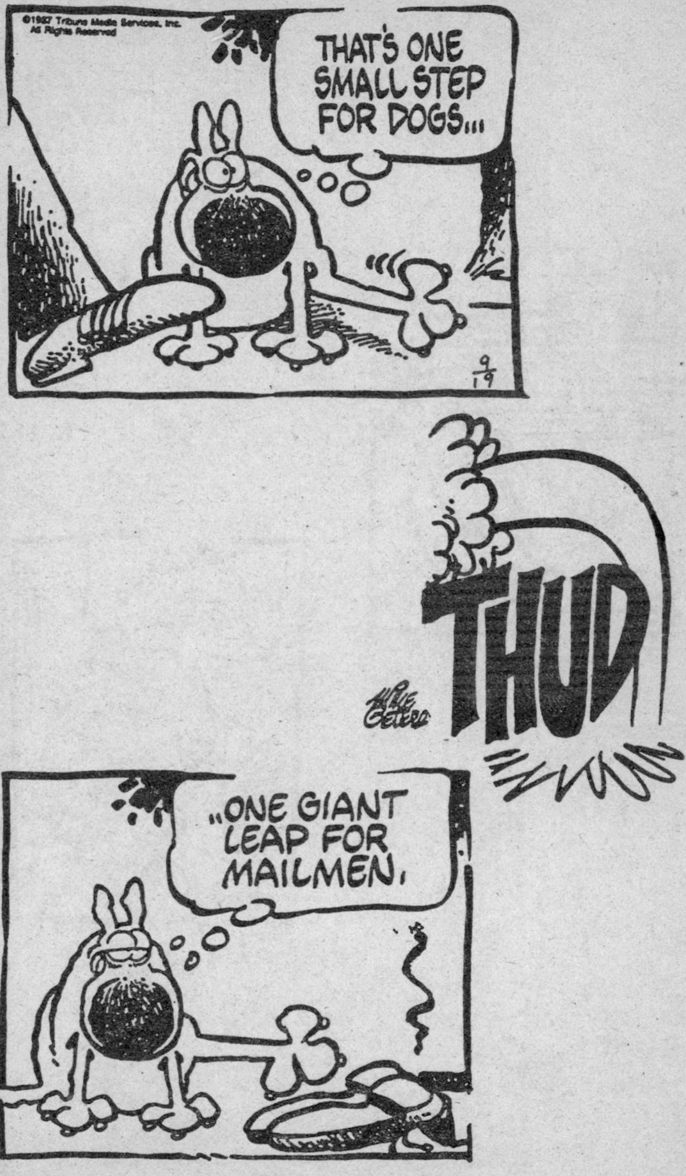
©1987 Tribune Media Services, Inc.
All Rights Reserved
THAT'S ONE SMALL STEP FOR DOGS...
9/19
THUD
...ONE GIANT LEAP FOR MAILMEN.

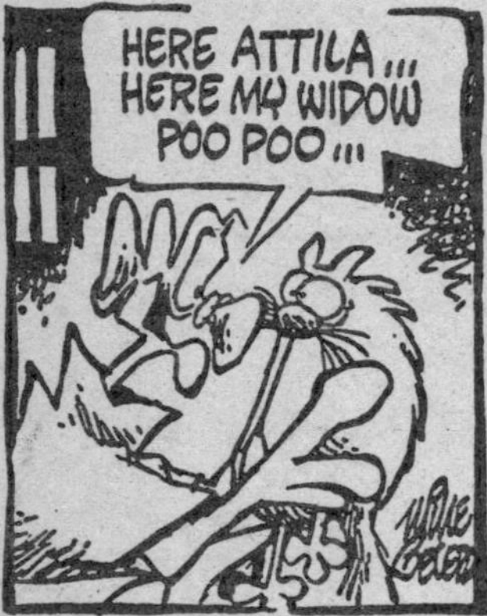
HERE ATTILA...
HERE MY WIDOW
POO POO...

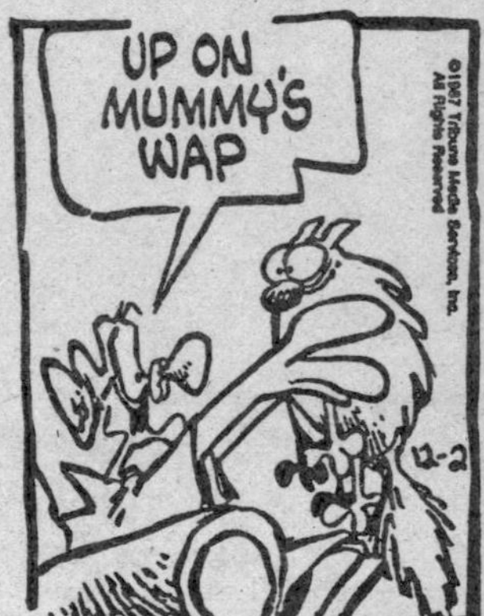
UP ON
MUMMY'S
WAP
©1987 Tribune Media Services, Inc.
All Rights Reserved
12-2

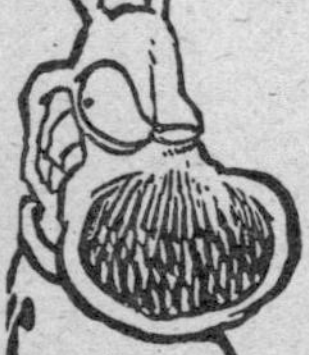

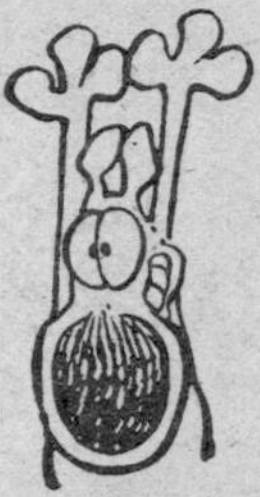

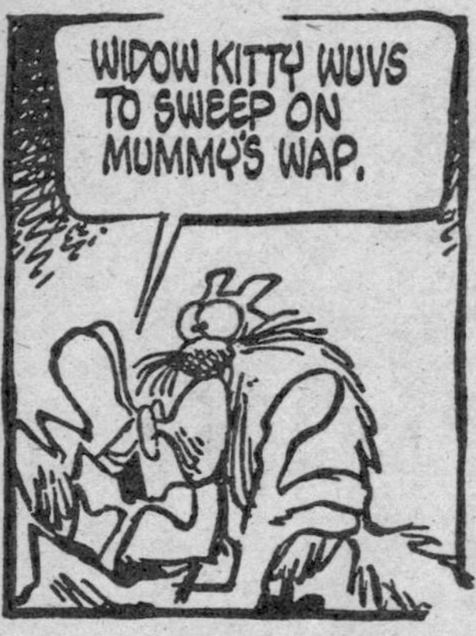
WIDOW KITTY WUVS TO SWEEP ON MUMMY'S WAP.

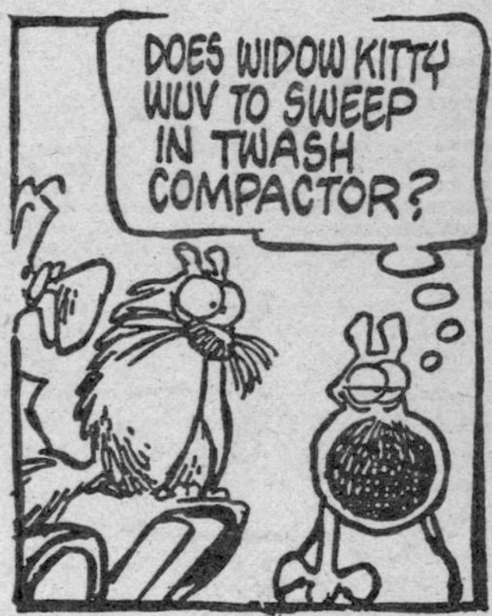
DOES WIDOW KITTY WUV TO SWEEP IN TWASH COMPACTOR?

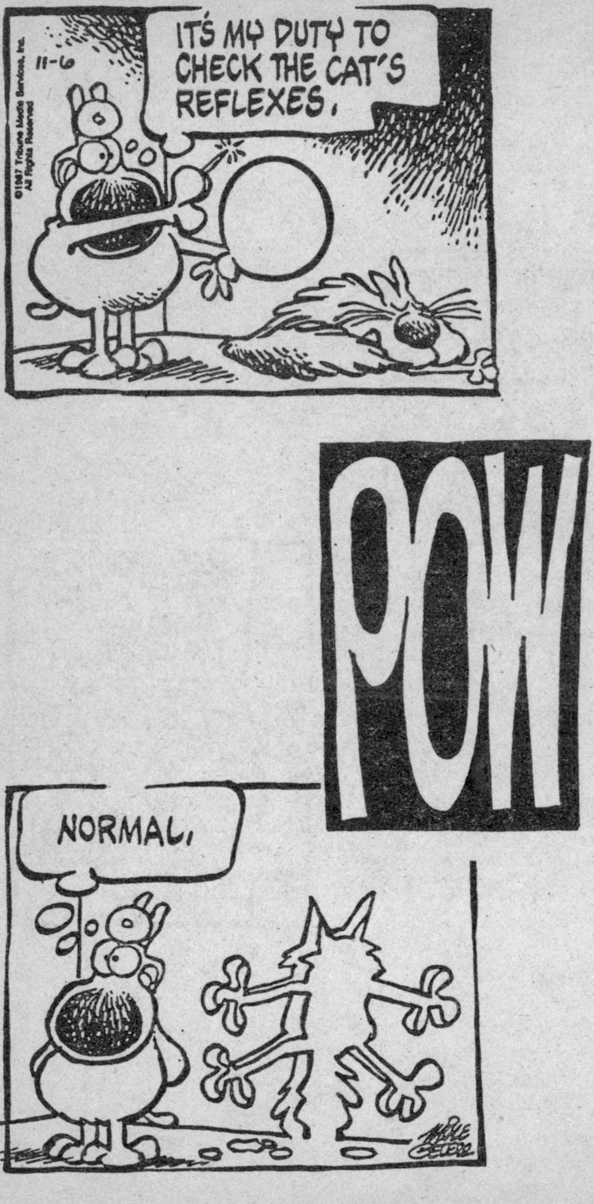
©1987 Tribune Media Services, Inc.
All Rights Reserved
11-6
IT'S MY DUTY TO CHECK THE CAT'S REFLEXES.
POW
NORMAL.

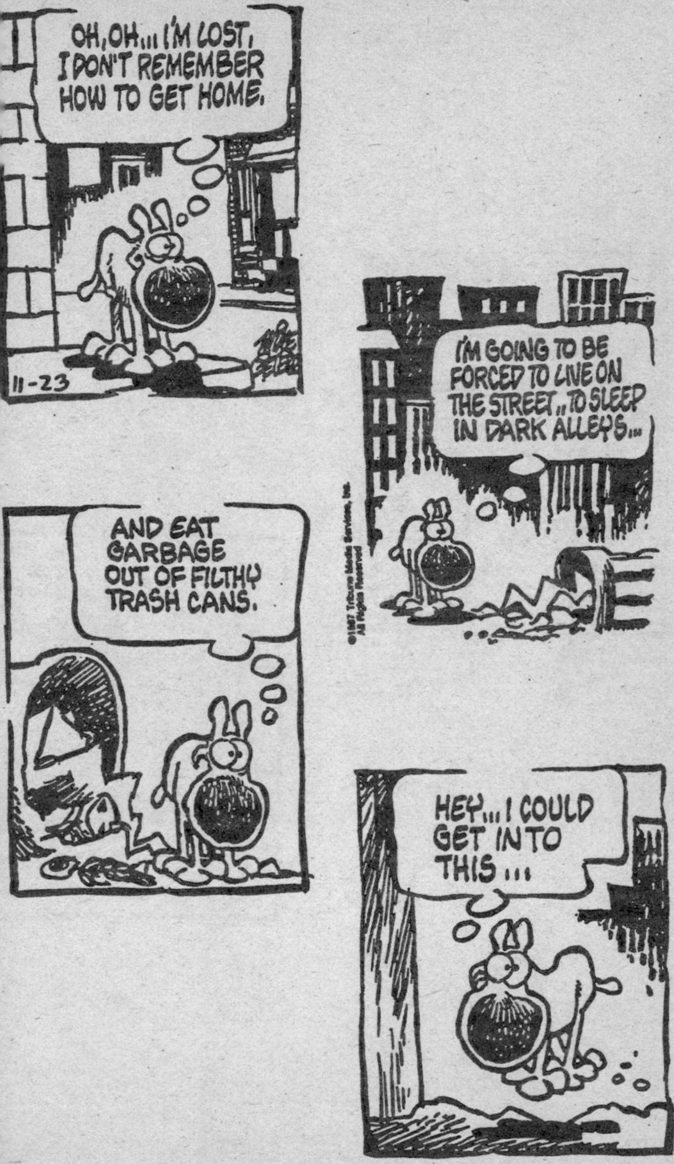
OH, OH... I'M LOST, I DON'T REMEMBER HOW TO GET HOME.
11-23
I'M GOING TO BE FORCED TO LIVE ON THE STREET.. TO SLEEP IN DARK ALLEYS...
AND EAT GARBAGE OUT OF FILTHY TRASH CANS.
HEY... I COULD GET INTO THIS...

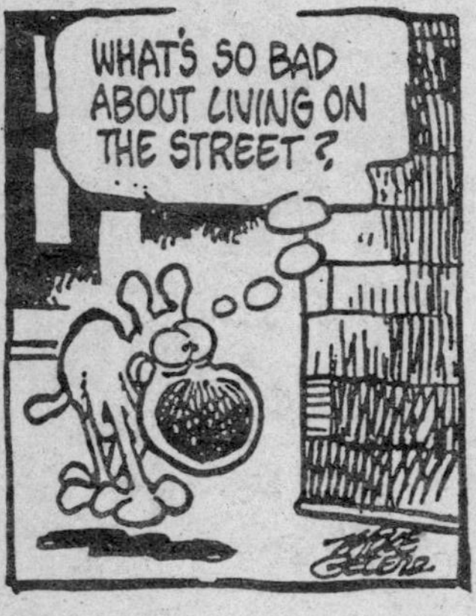
WHAT'S SO BAD ABOUT LIVING ON THE STREET?

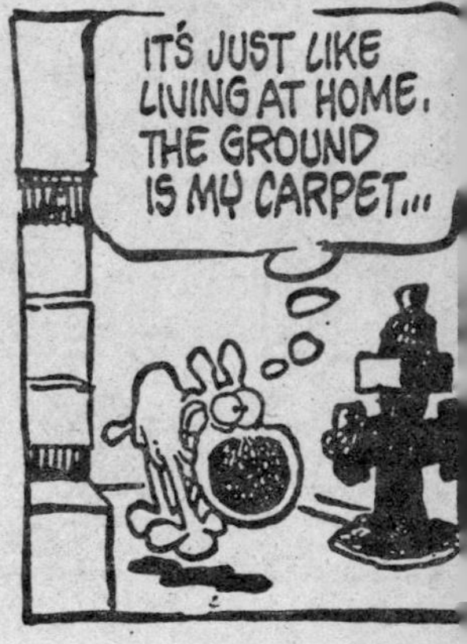
IT'S JUST LIKE LIVING AT HOME. THE GROUND IS MY CARPET...

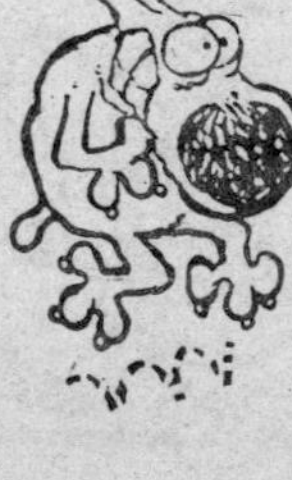

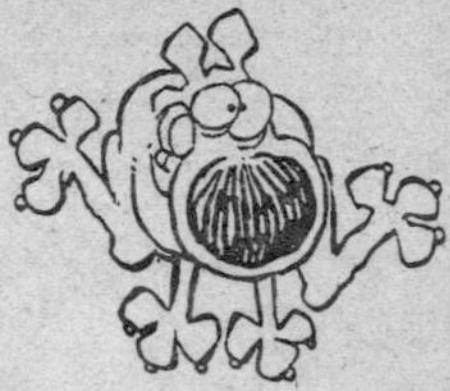

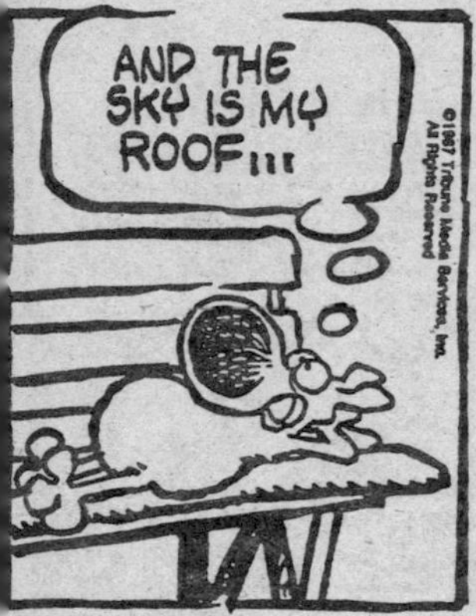
AND THE SKY IS MY ROOF...
©1987 Tribune Media Services, Inc.
All Rights Reserved

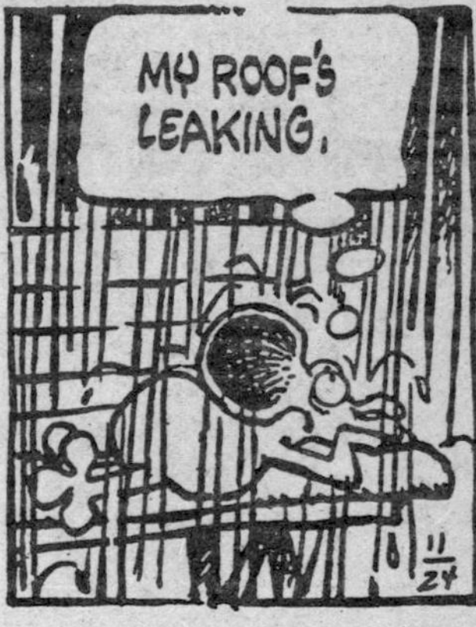
MY ROOF'S LEAKING.
11/24

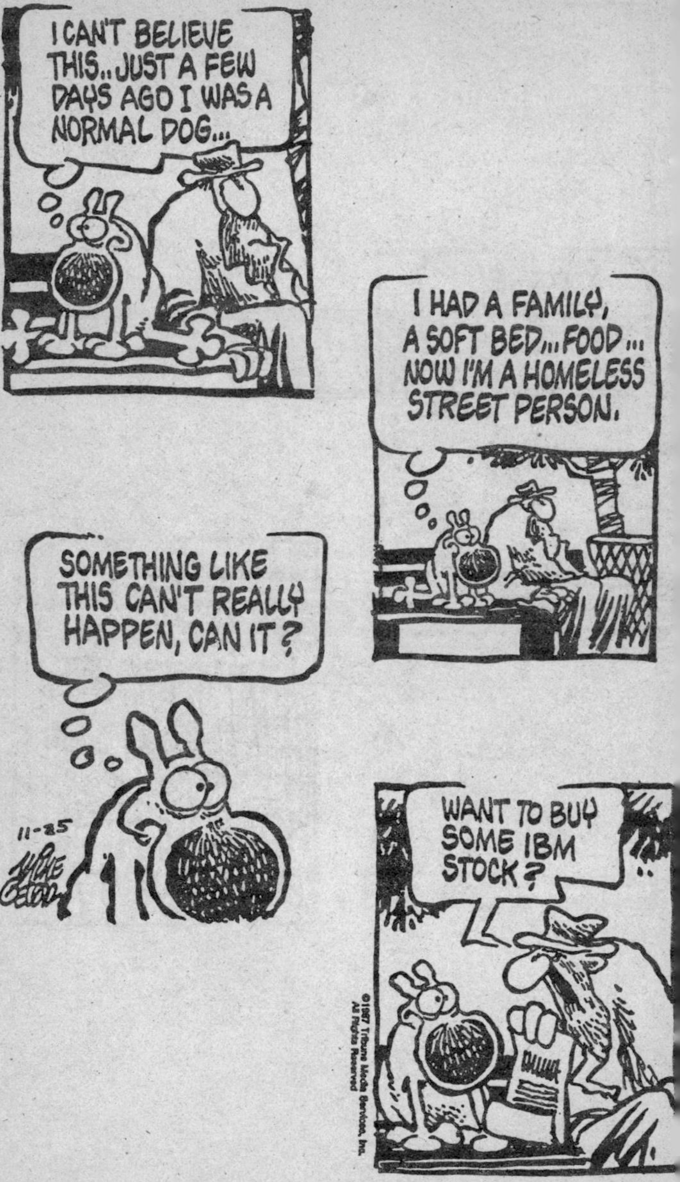
I CAN'T BELIEVE THIS.. JUST A FEW DAYS AGO I WAS A NORMAL DOG...
I HAD A FAMILY, A SOFT BED... FOOD... NOW I'M A HOMELESS STREET PERSON.
SOMETHING LIKE THIS CAN'T REALLY HAPPEN, CAN IT?
11-25
WANT TO BUY SOME IBM STOCK?
©1987 Tribune Media Services, Inc.
All Rights Reserved

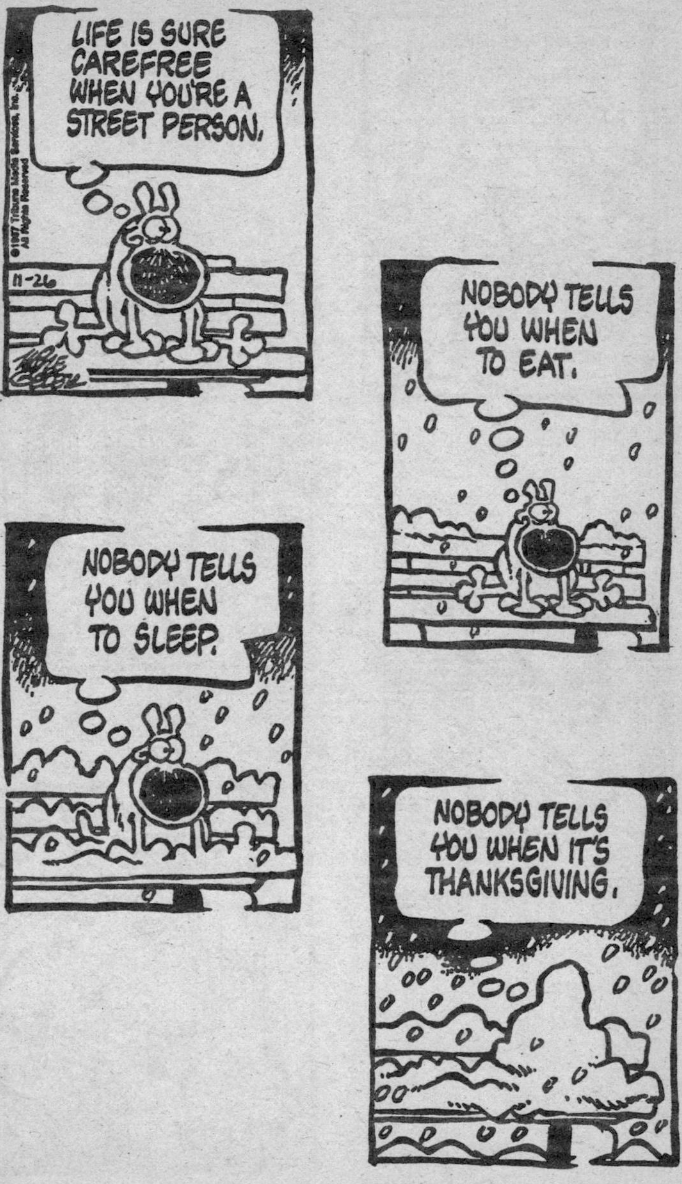
LIFE IS SURE CAREFREE WHEN YOU'RE A STREET PERSON.
©1997 Tribune Media Services, Inc. All Rights Reserved
11-26
NOBODY TELLS YOU WHEN TO EAT.
NOBODY TELLS YOU WHEN TO SLEEP.
NOBODY TELLS YOU WHEN IT'S THANKSGIVING.

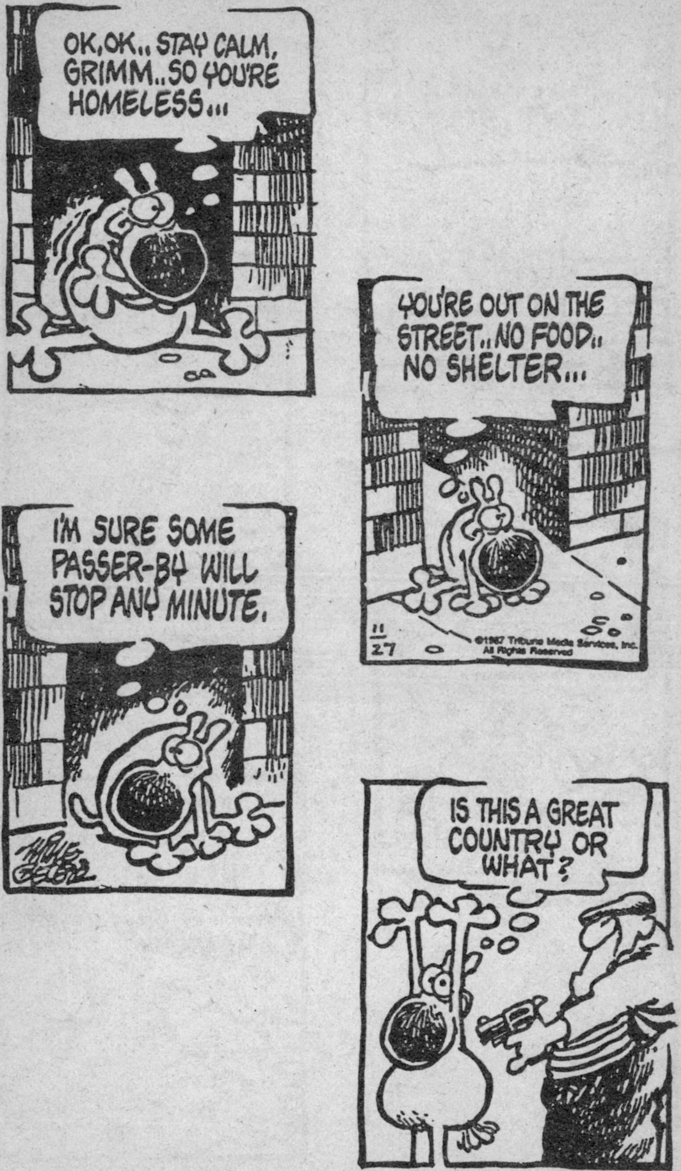

OK, OK.. STAY CALM, GRIMM.. SO YOU'RE HOMELESS...
YOU'RE OUT ON THE STREET.. NO FOOD.. NO SHELTER...
11 27
©1987 Tribune Media Services, Inc. All Rights Reserved
I'M SURE SOME PASSER-BY WILL STOP ANY MINUTE.
IS THIS A GREAT COUNTRY OR WHAT?

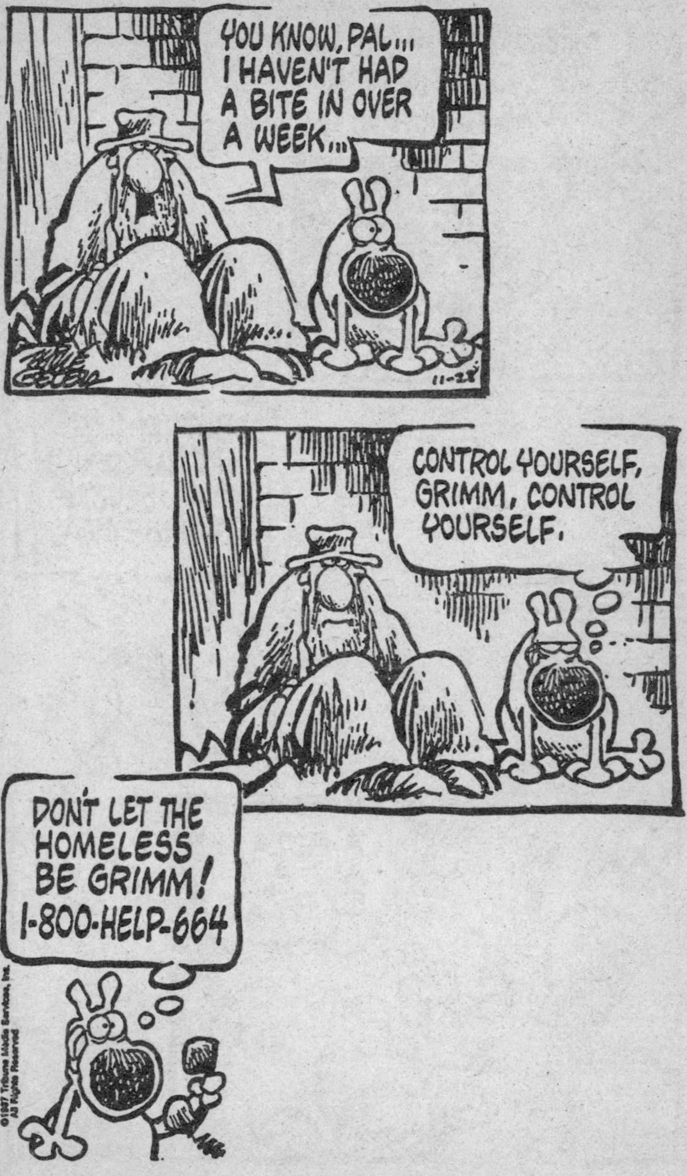
YOU KNOW, PAL... I HAVEN'T HAD A BITE IN OVER A WEEK...
11-28
CONTROL YOURSELF, GRIMM, CONTROL YOURSELF.
DON'T LET THE HOMELESS BE GRIMM! 1-800-HELP-664

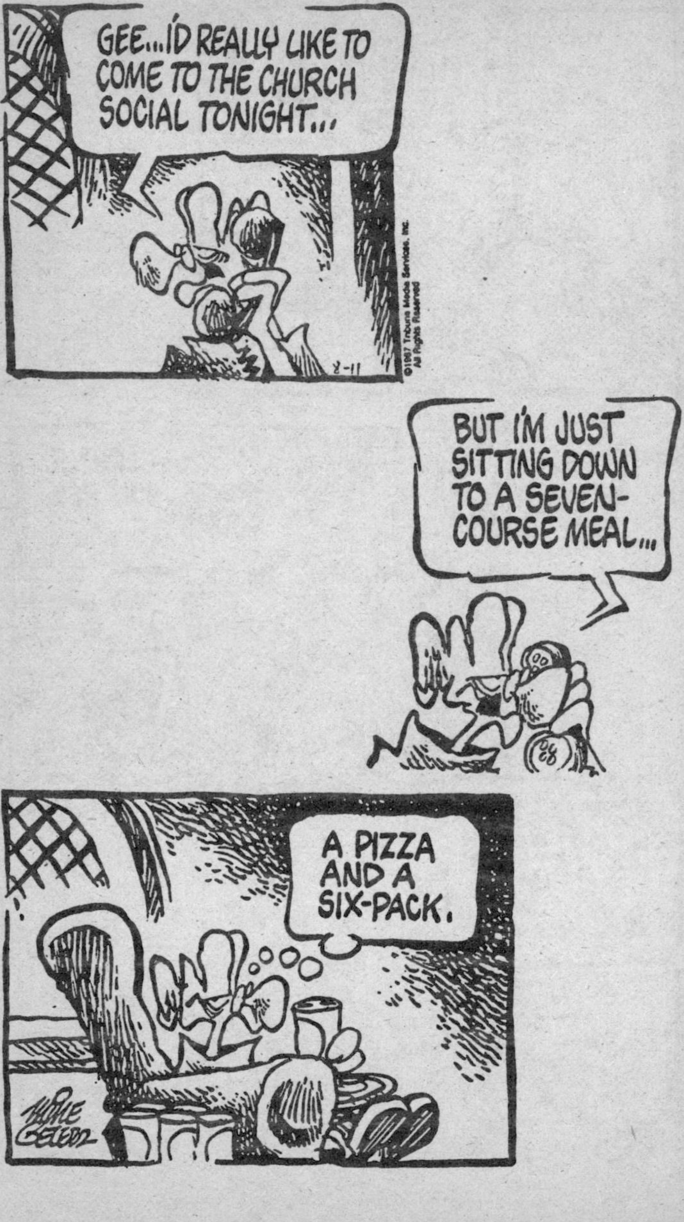
GEE...I'D REALLY LIKE TO COME TO THE CHURCH SOCIAL TONIGHT...
©1987 Tribune Media Services, Inc. All Rights Reserved
BUT I'M JUST SITTING DOWN TO A SEVEN-COURSE MEAL...
A PIZZA AND A SIX-PACK.

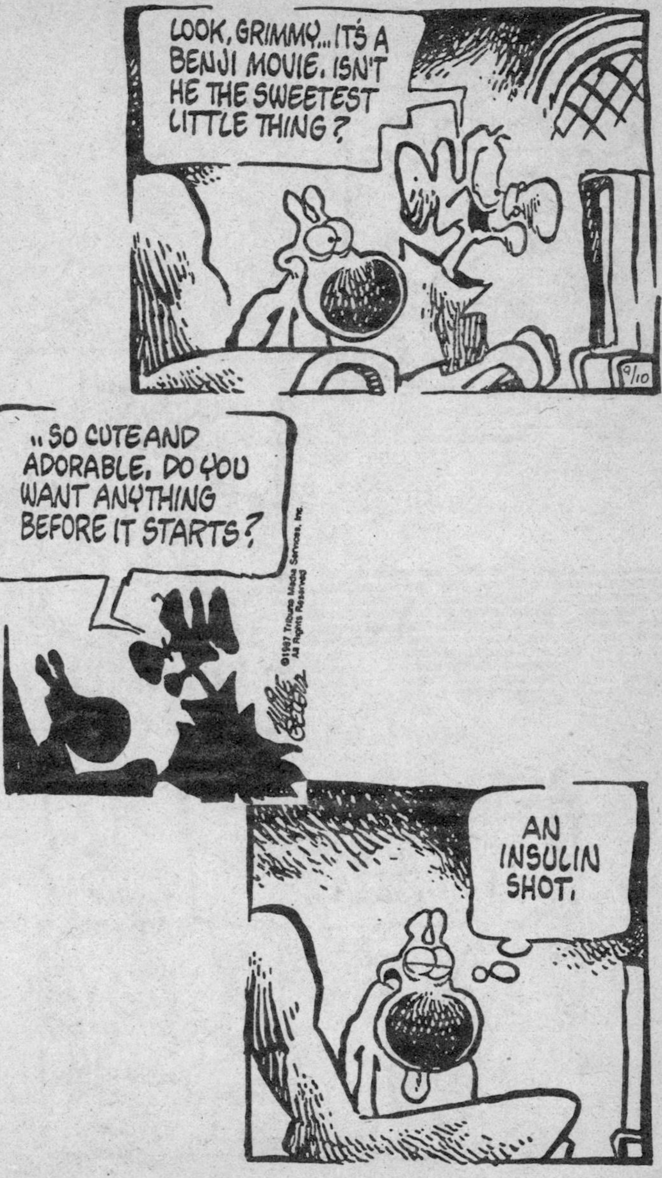

LOOK, GRIMMY... IT'S A BENJI MOVIE. ISN'T HE THE SWEETEST LITTLE THING?
9/10
.. SO CUTE AND ADORABLE. DO YOU WANT ANYTHING BEFORE IT STARTS?
©1987 Tribune Media Services, Inc.
All Rights Reserved
AN INSULIN SHOT.

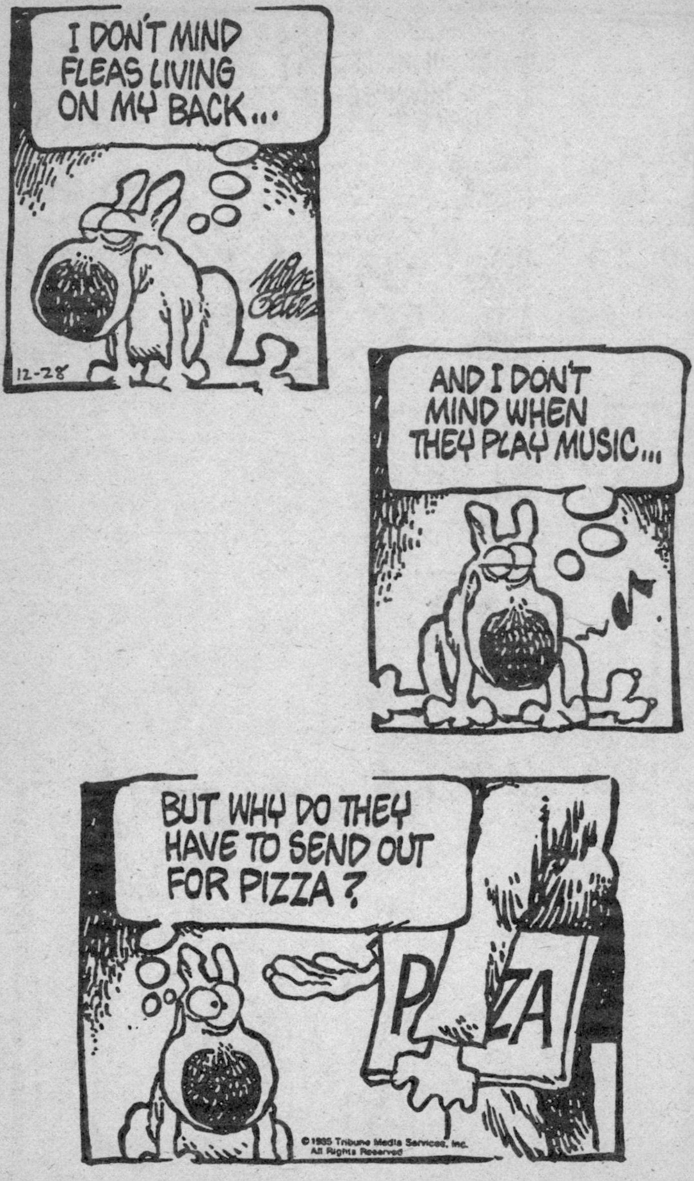
I DON'T MIND FLEAS LIVING ON MY BACK...
12-28
AND I DON'T MIND WHEN THEY PLAY MUSIC...
BUT WHY DO THEY HAVE TO SEND OUT FOR PIZZA?
P ZA
© 1985 Tribune Media Services, Inc.
All Rights Reserved

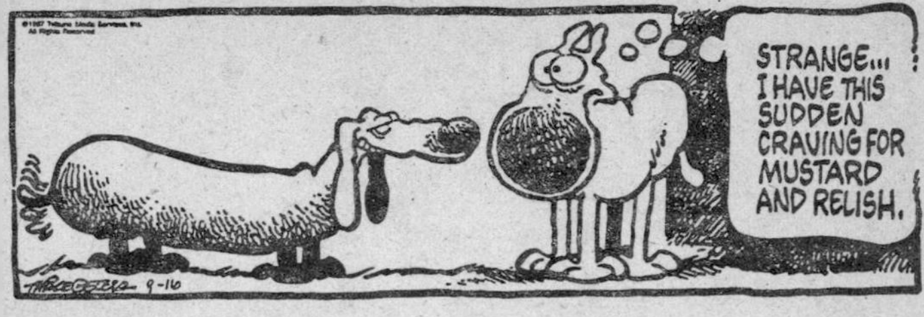
STRANGE... I HAVE THIS SUDDEN CRAVING FOR MUSTARD AND RELISH.

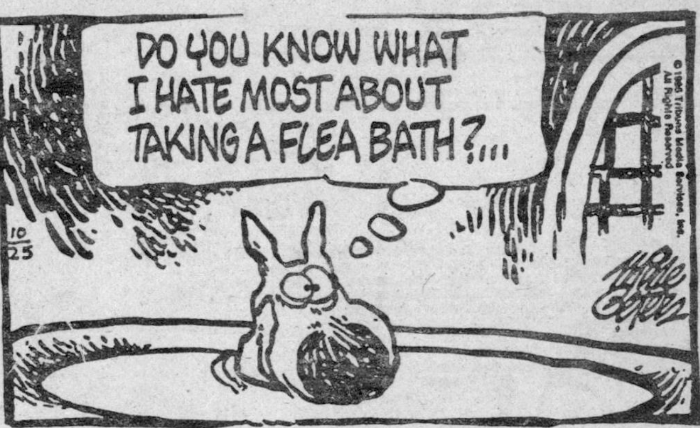
DO YOU KNOW WHAT I HATE MOST ABOUT TAKING A FLEA BATH?...

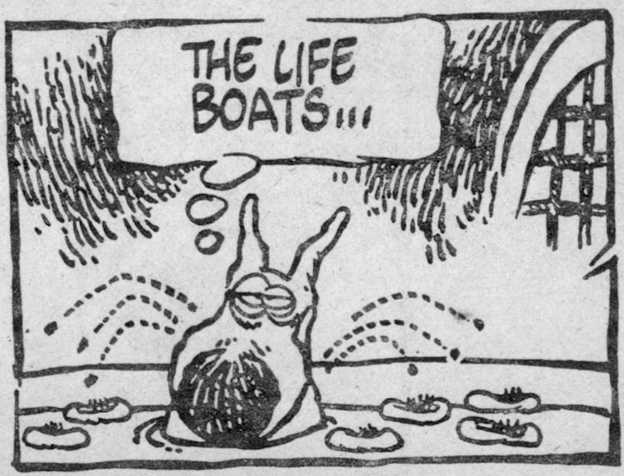
THE LIFE BOATS...

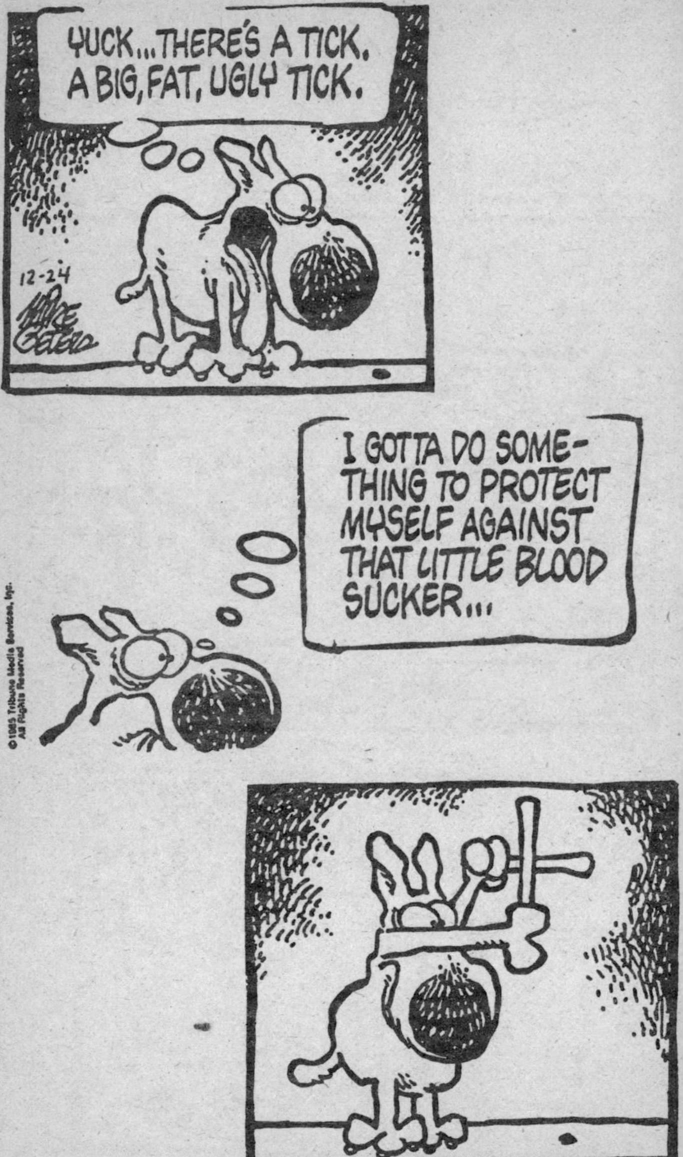
YUCK...THERE'S A TICK. A BIG, FAT, UGLY TICK.
12-24
I GOTTA DO SOME-THING TO PROTECT MYSELF AGAINST THAT LITTLE BLOOD SUCKER...

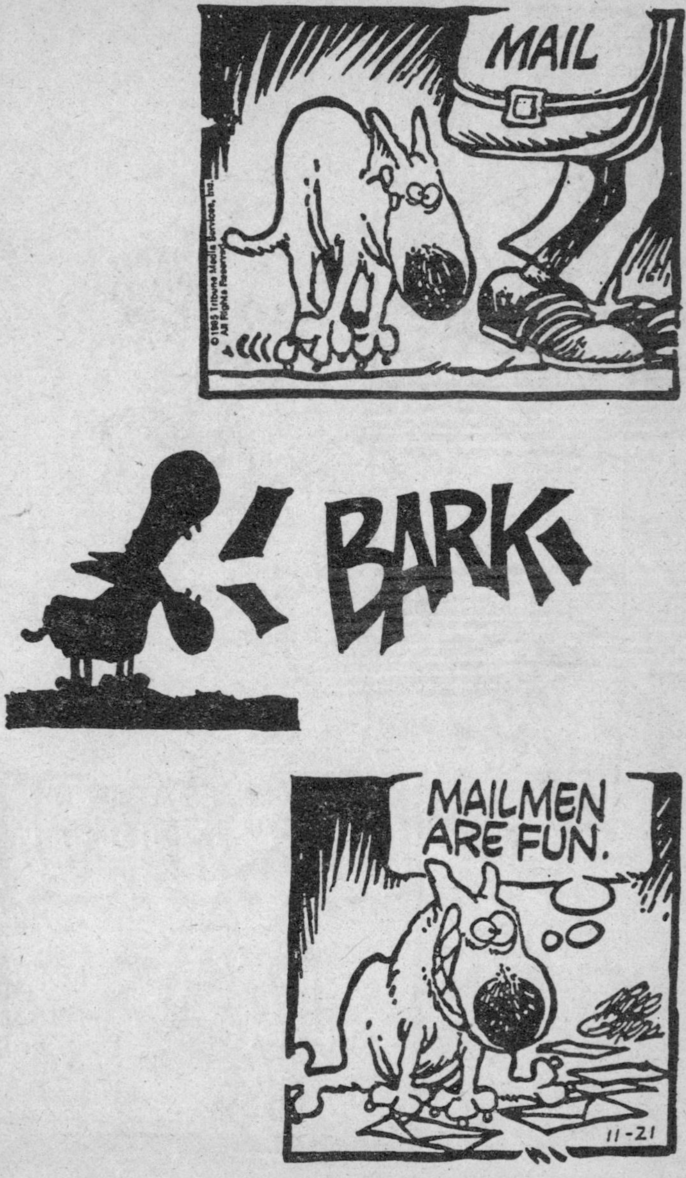
MAIL
©1985 Tribune Media Services, Inc.
All Rights Reserved
BARK
MAILMEN ARE FUN.
11-21

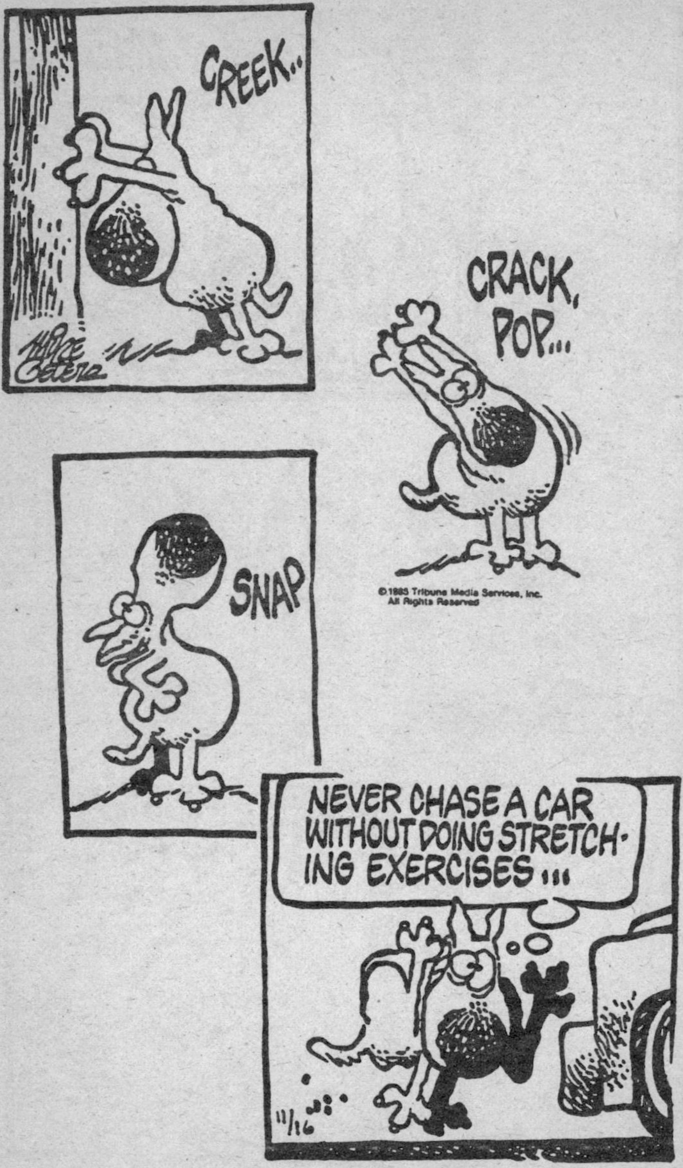
CREEK..
CRACK, POP...
SNAP
NEVER CHASE A CAR WITHOUT DOING STRETCH-ING EXERCISES...
11/16

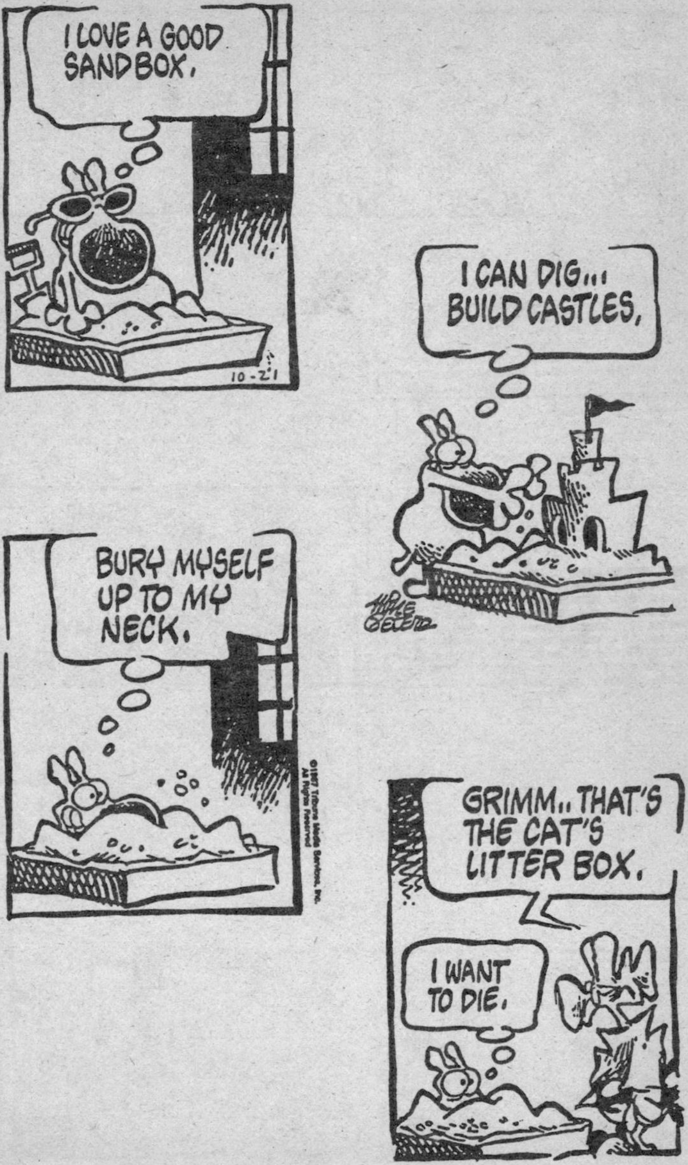
I LOVE A GOOD SANDBOX.
10-21
I CAN DIG... BUILD CASTLES.
BURY MYSELF UP TO MY NECK.
©1987 Tribune Media Services, Inc. All Rights Reserved
GRIMM.. THAT'S THE CAT'S LITTER BOX.
I WANT TO DIE.

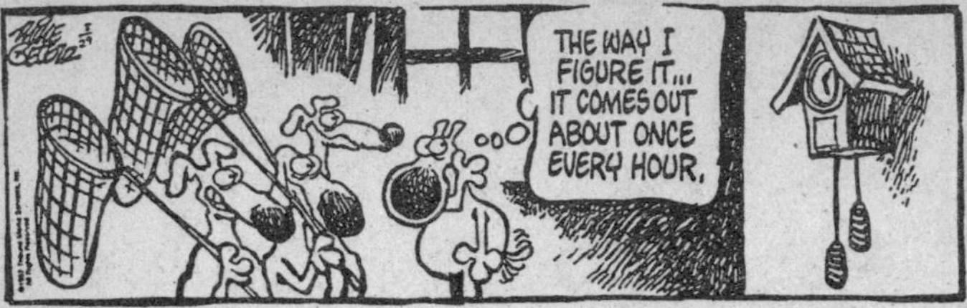
THE WAY I FIGURE IT... IT COMES OUT ABOUT ONCE EVERY HOUR.

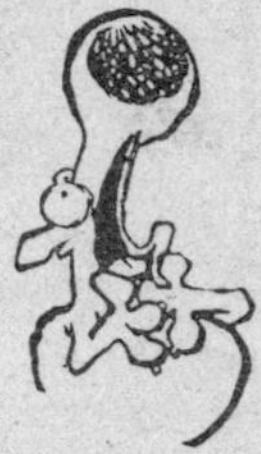

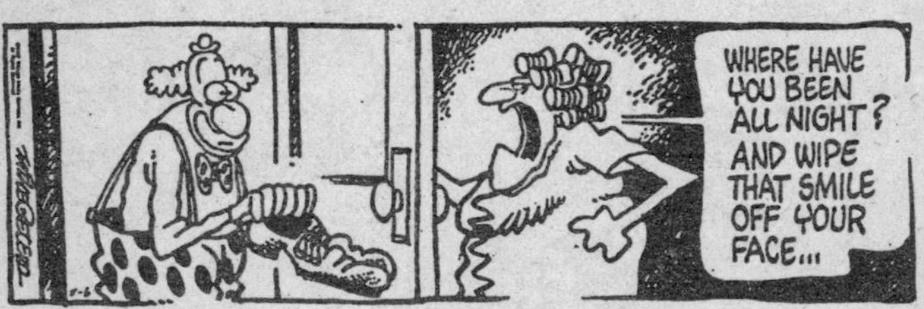
WHERE HAVE YOU BEEN ALL NIGHT? AND WIPE THAT SMILE OFF YOUR FACE...

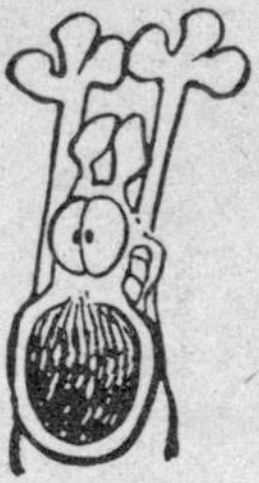

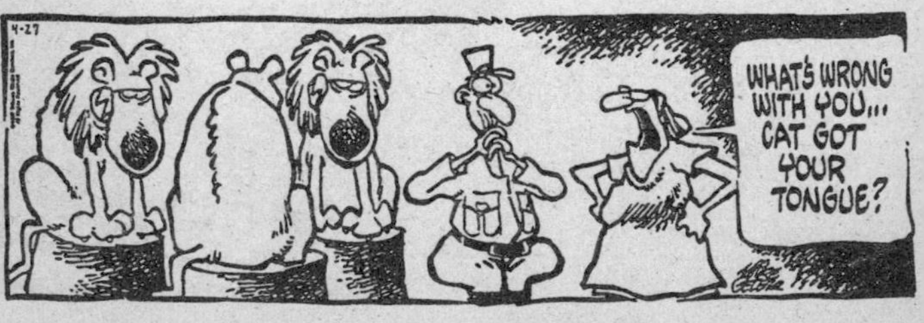
WHAT'S WRONG WITH YOU... CAT GOT YOUR TONGUE?

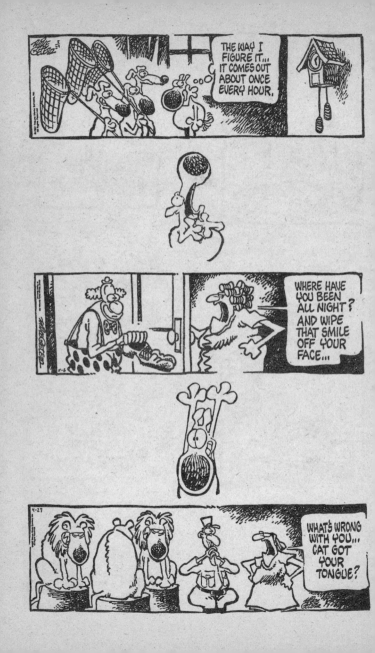

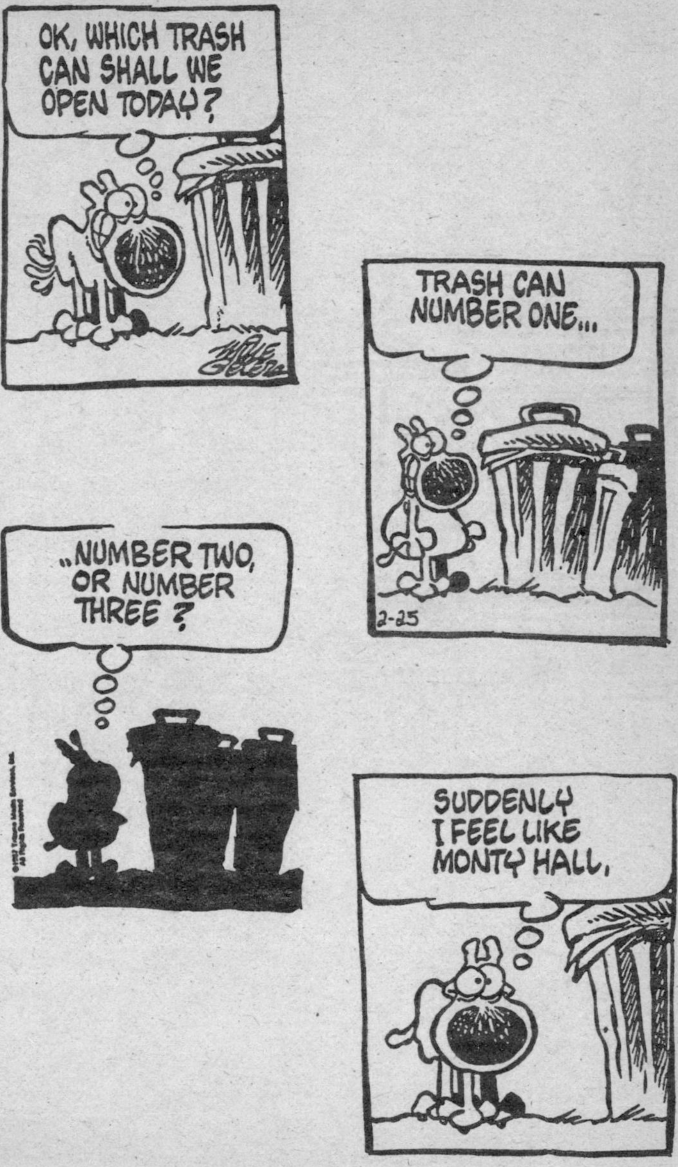
OK, WHICH TRASH CAN SHALL WE OPEN TODAY?
TRASH CAN NUMBER ONE...
2-25
..NUMBER TWO, OR NUMBER THREE?
SUDDENLY I FEEL LIKE MONTY HALL.

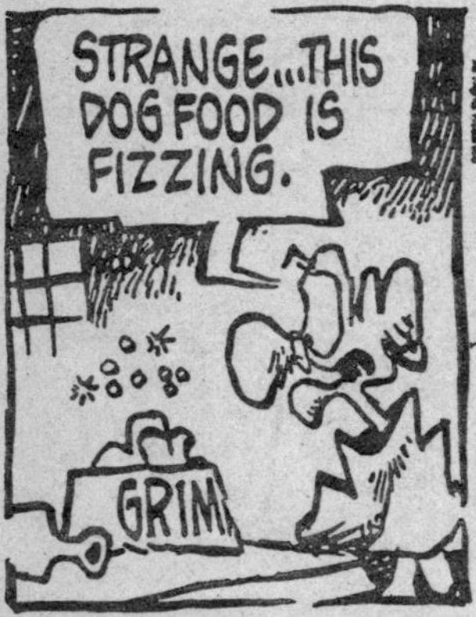
STRANGE...THIS DOG FOOD IS FIZZING.
GRIM

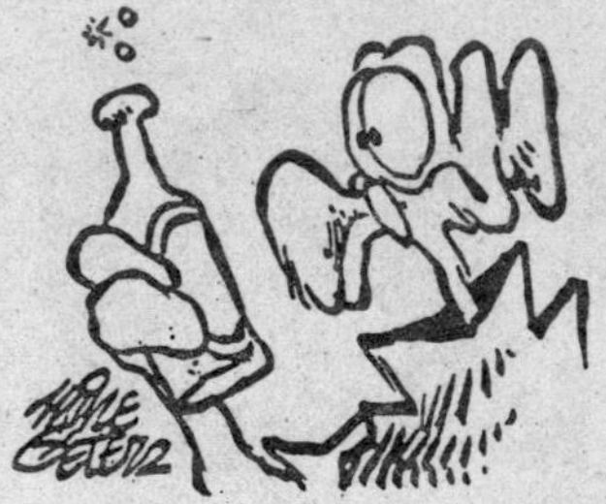

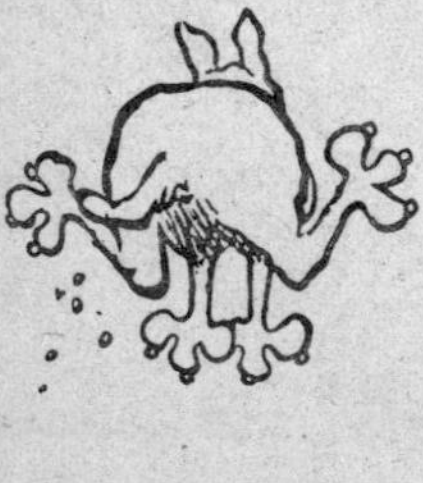

GRIMM.. YOU PUT PERRIER WATER IN YOUR GRAVY TRAIN!

I'M JUST AN '80'S KIND OF GUY.

GRIM

2-21

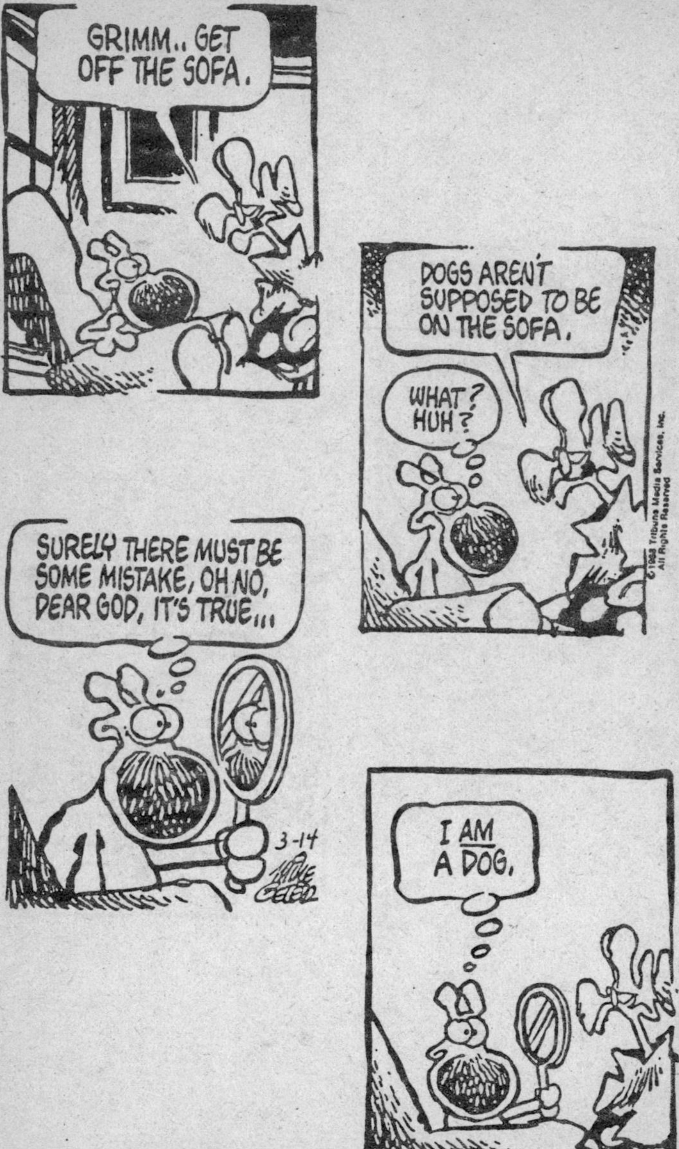
GRIMM.. GET OFF THE SOFA.
DOGS AREN'T SUPPOSED TO BE ON THE SOFA.
WHAT? HUH?
SURELY THERE MUST BE SOME MISTAKE, OH NO, DEAR GOD, IT'S TRUE...
3-14
I AM A DOG.

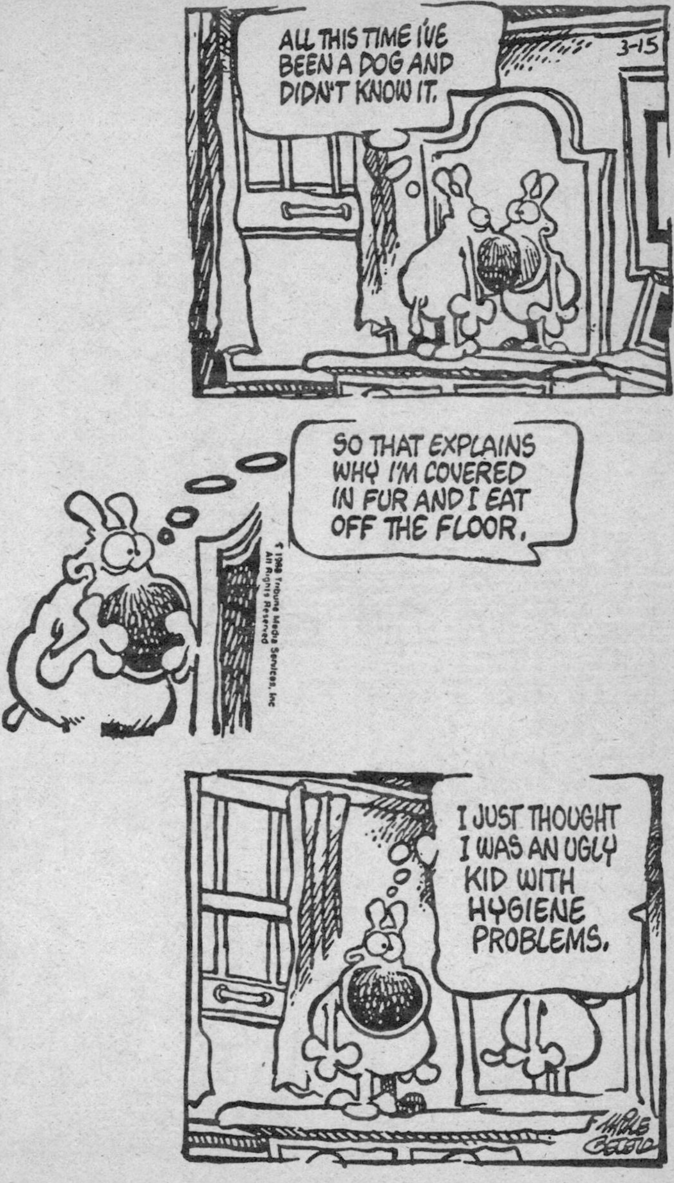
3-15
ALL THIS TIME I'VE BEEN A DOG AND DIDN'T KNOW IT.
SO THAT EXPLAINS WHY I'M COVERED IN FUR AND I EAT OFF THE FLOOR.
© 1988 Tribune Media Services, Inc
All Rights Reserved
I JUST THOUGHT I WAS AN UGLY KID WITH HYGIENE PROBLEMS.

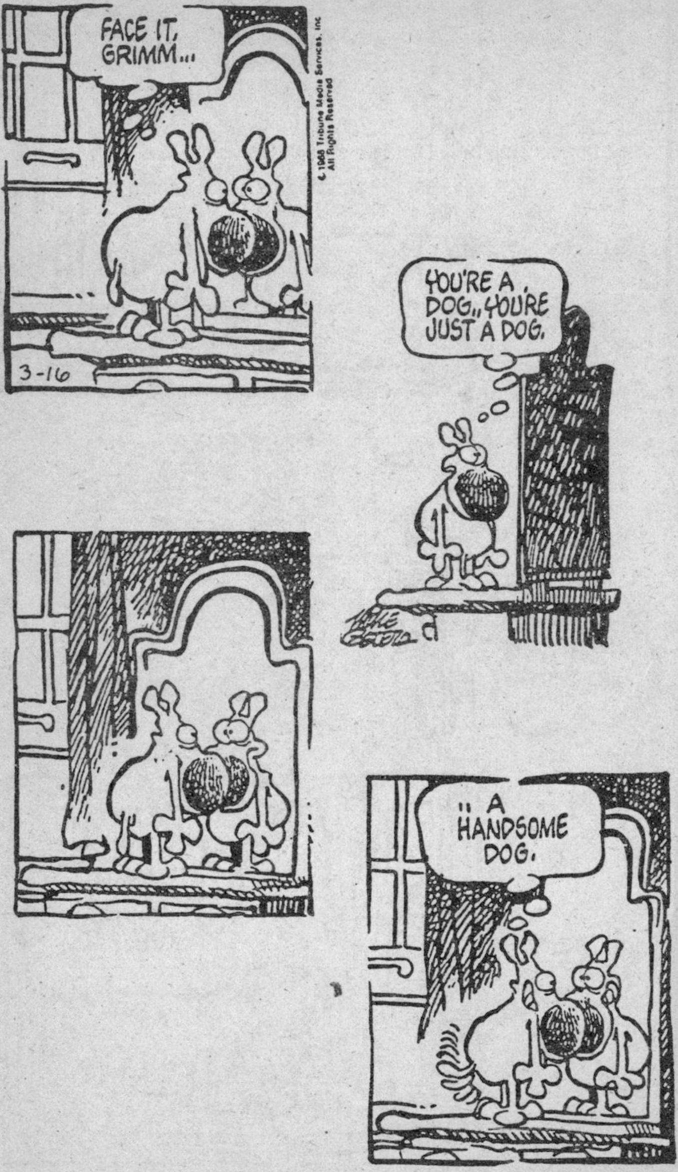
FACE IT, GRIMM...
3-16
© 1988 Tribune Media Services, Inc
All Rights Reserved
YOU'RE A DOG,, YOU'RE JUST A DOG.
.. A HANDSOME DOG.

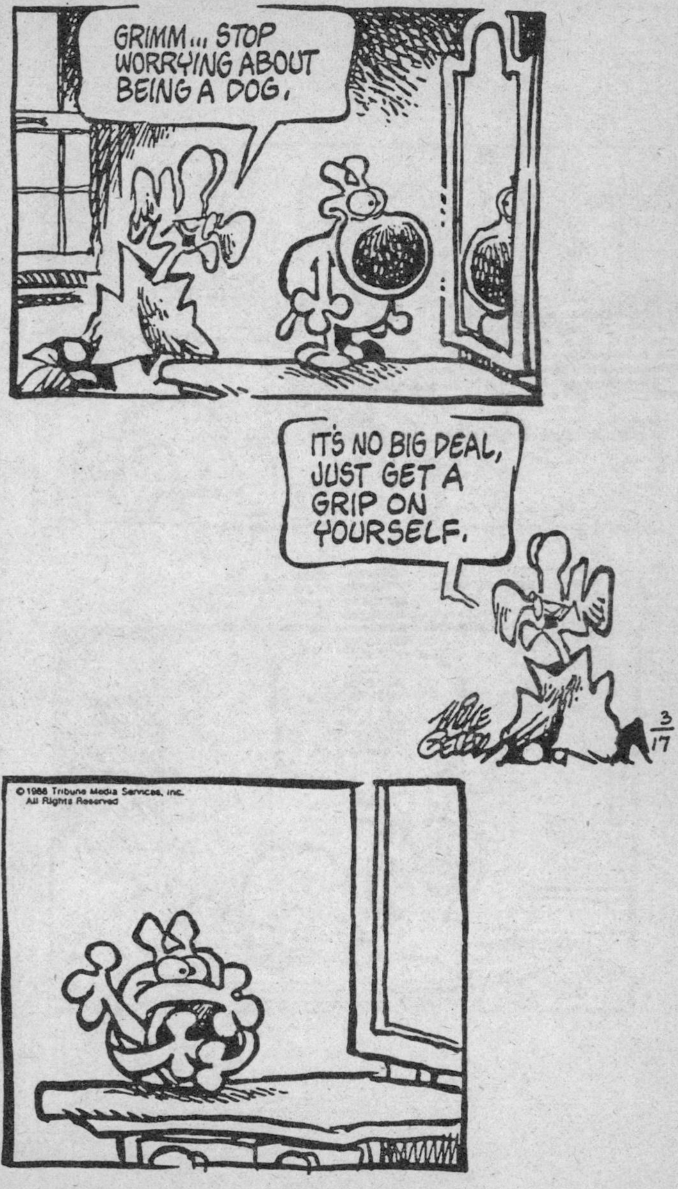
GRIMM... STOP WORRYING ABOUT BEING A DOG.
IT'S NO BIG DEAL, JUST GET A GRIP ON YOURSELF.
3/17

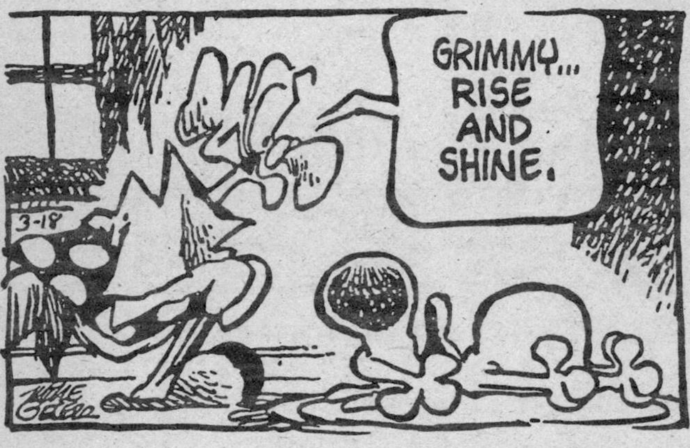
3-18
GRIMMY... RISE AND SHINE.

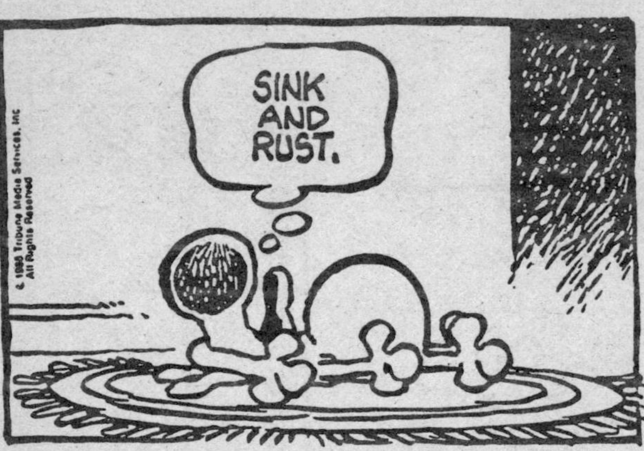
SINK AND RUST.

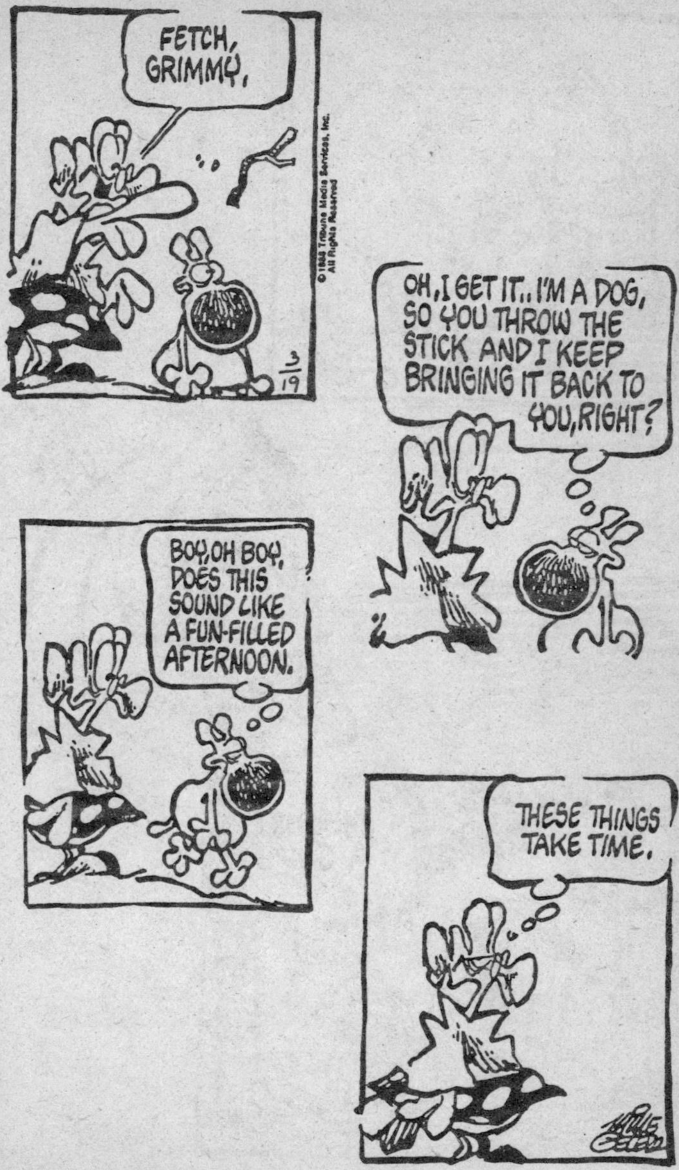
FETCH, GRIMMY.
3/19
OH, I GET IT.. I'M A DOG, SO YOU THROW THE STICK AND I KEEP BRINGING IT BACK TO YOU, RIGHT?
BOY, OH BOY, DOES THIS SOUND LIKE A FUN-FILLED AFTERNOON.
THESE THINGS TAKE TIME.

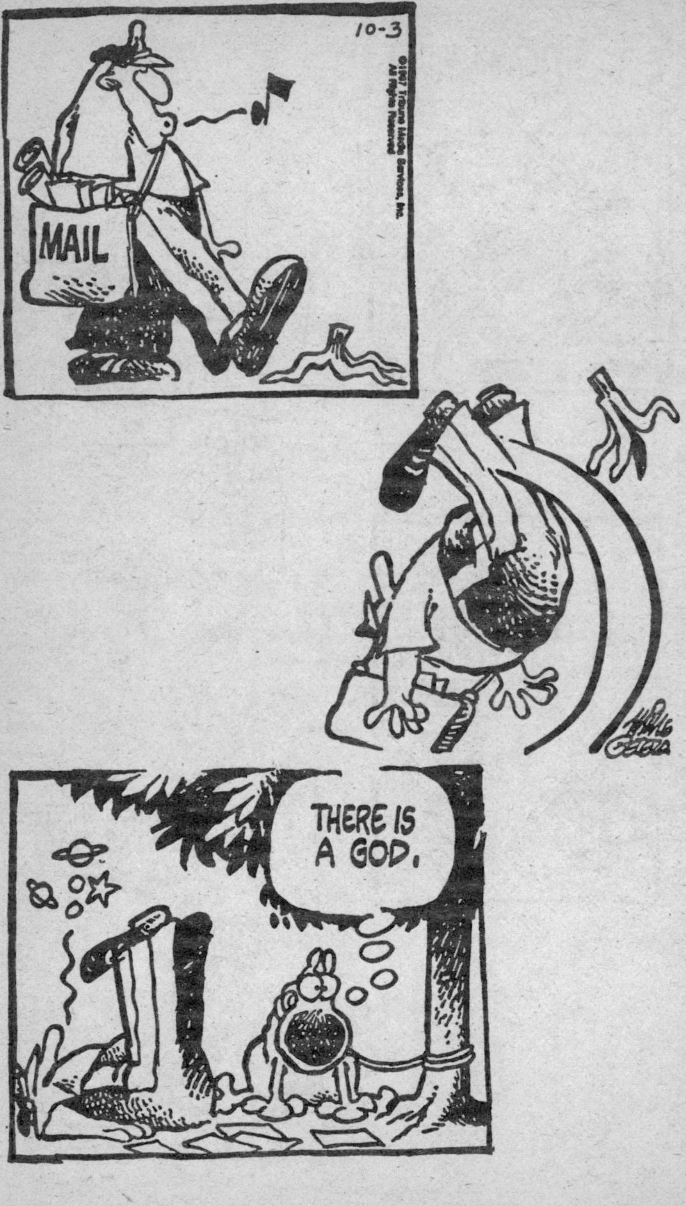
10-3
©1987 Tribune Media Services, Inc.
All Rights Reserved
MAIL
THERE IS A GOD.

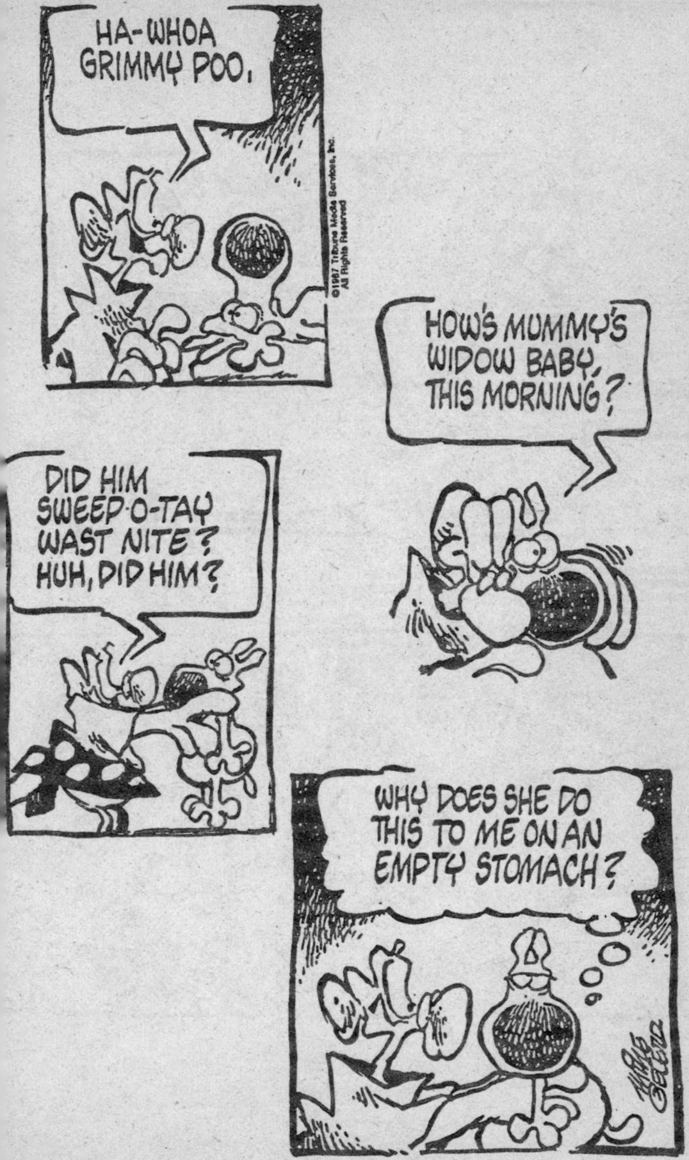
HA-WHOA GRIMMY POO.
©1987 Tribune Media Services, Inc. All Rights Reserved
HOW'S MUMMY'S WIDOW BABY, THIS MORNING?
DID HIM SWEEP-O-TAY WAST NITE? HUH, DID HIM?
WHY DOES SHE DO THIS TO ME ON AN EMPTY STOMACH?

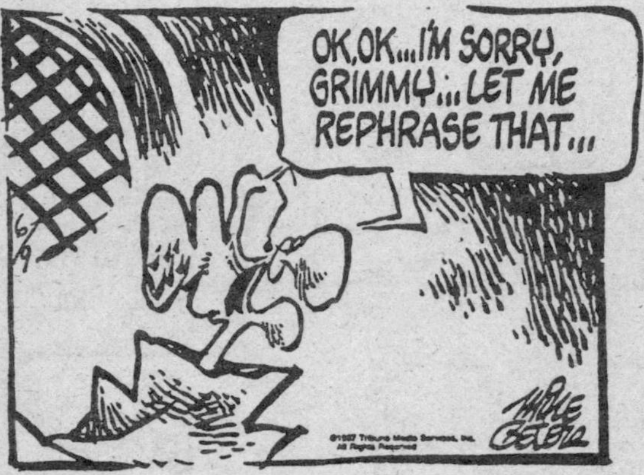
OK,OK...I'M SORRY, GRIMMY... LET ME REPHRASE THAT...
MIKE PETERS

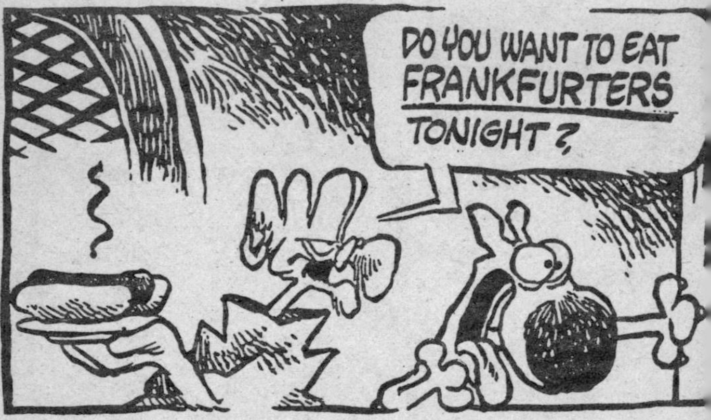
DO YOU WANT TO EAT FRANKFURTERS TONIGHT?

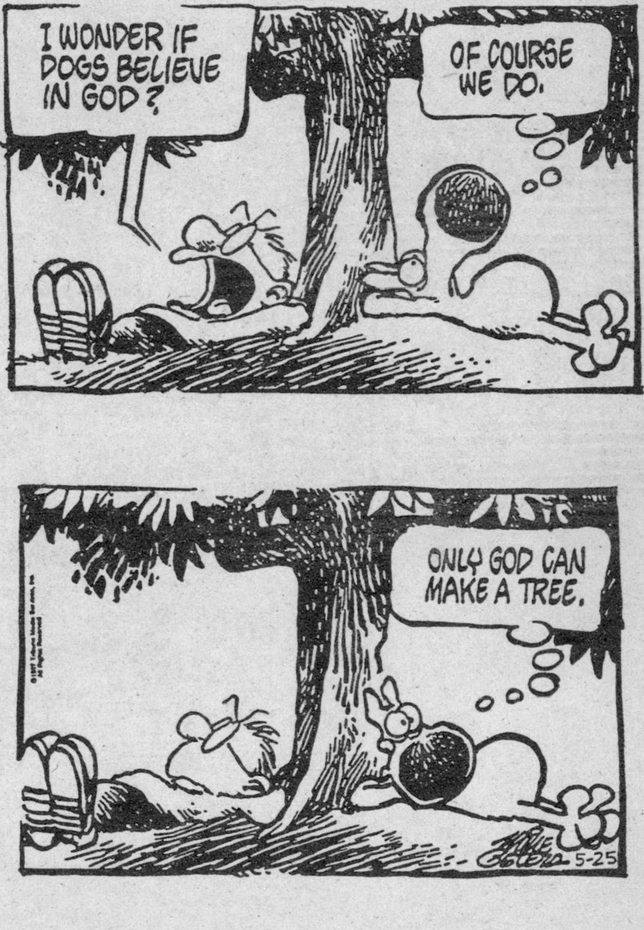
I WONDER IF DOGS BELIEVE IN GOD?
OF COURSE WE DO.
ONLY GOD CAN MAKE A TREE.
5-25

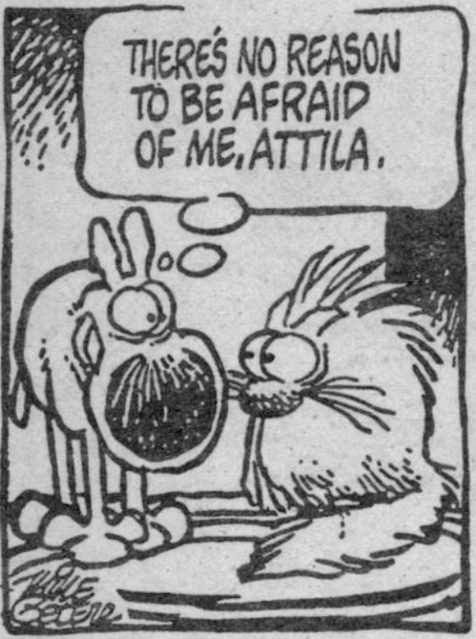
THERE'S NO REASON TO BE AFRAID OF ME, ATTILA.

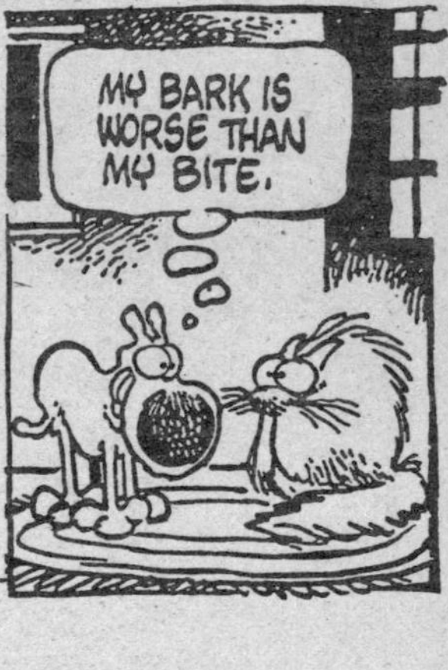
MY BARK IS WORSE THAN MY BITE.

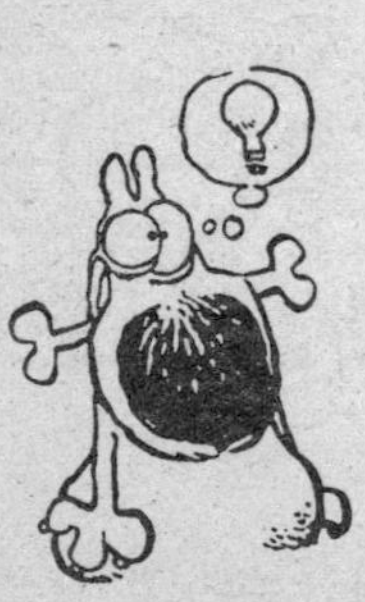

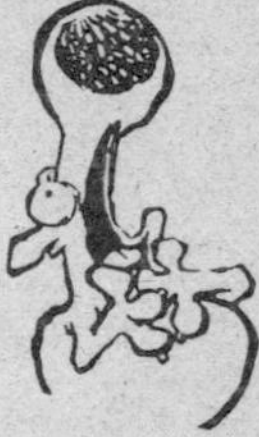

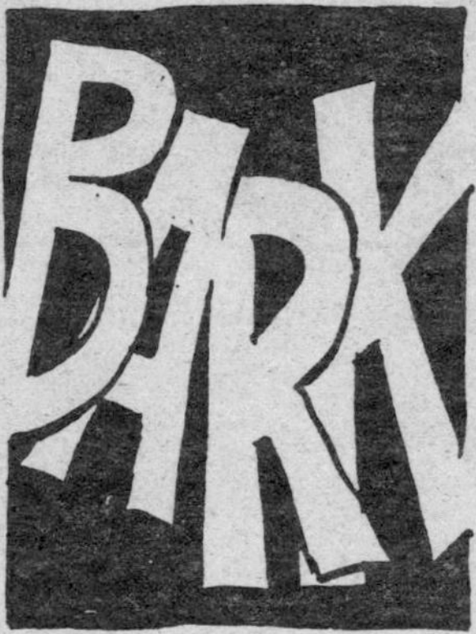
BARK

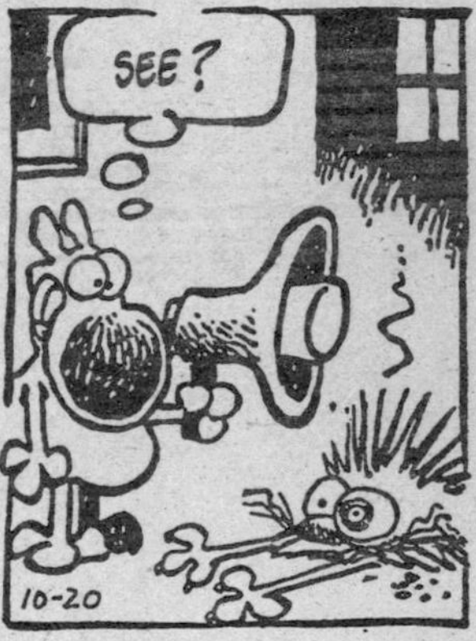
SEE?
10-20

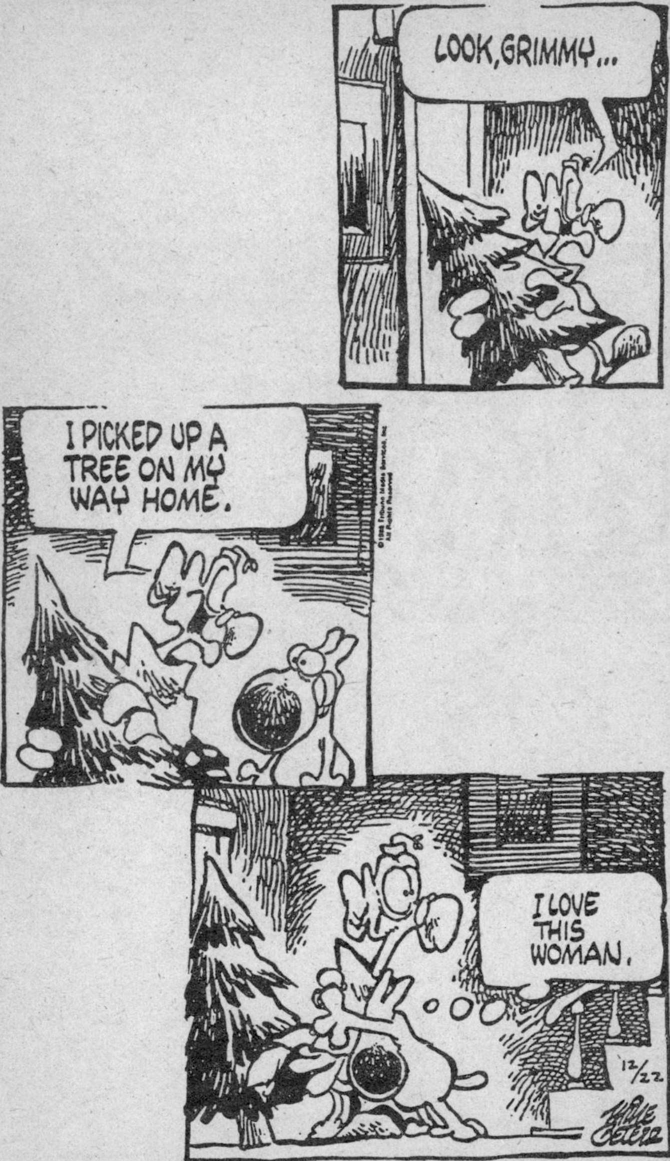
LOOK, GRIMMY...
I PICKED UP A TREE ON MY WAY HOME.
I LOVE THIS WOMAN.
12/22

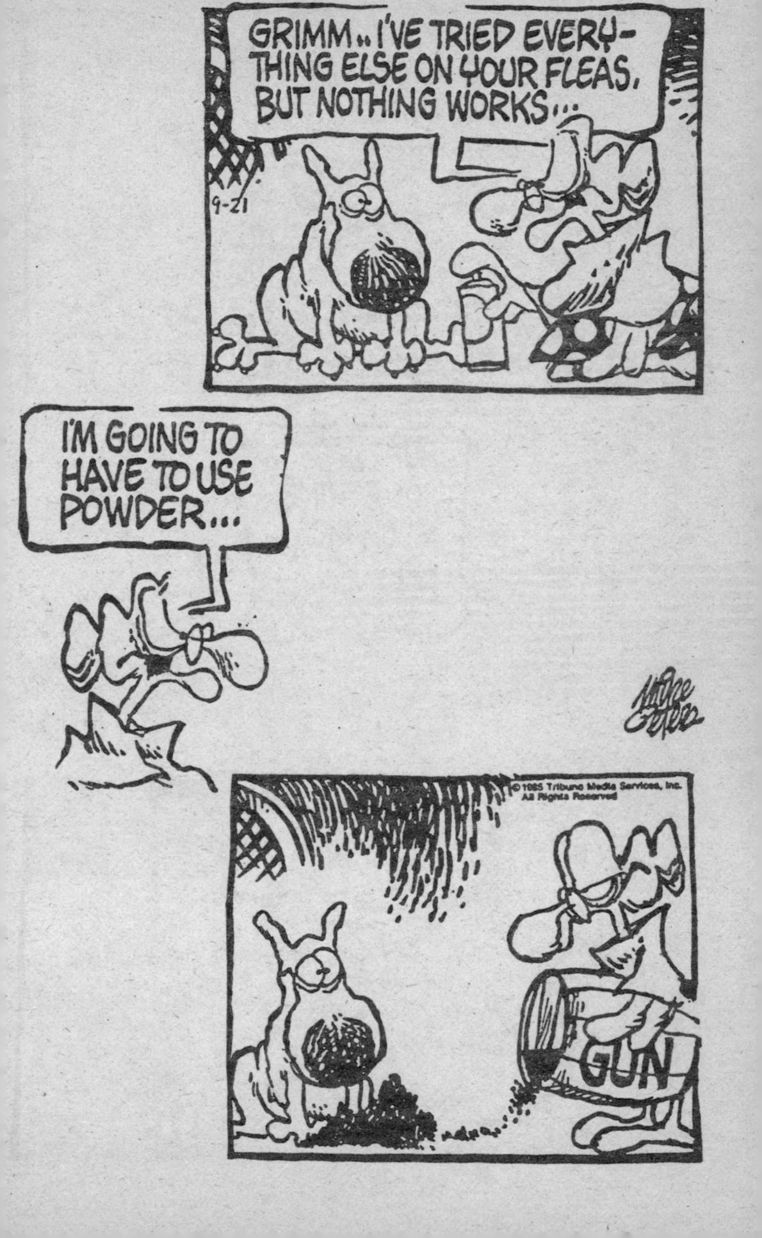

9-21
GRIMM.. I'VE TRIED EVERYTHING ELSE ON YOUR FLEAS, BUT NOTHING WORKS...
I'M GOING TO HAVE TO USE POWDER...
GUN

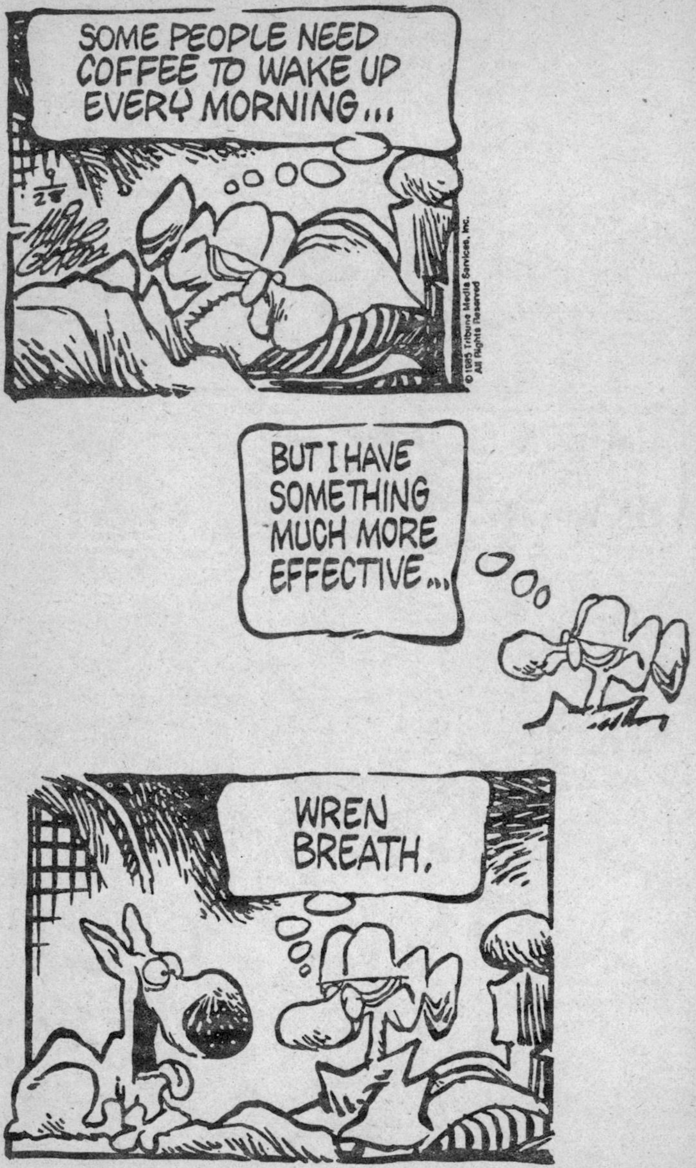

SOME PEOPLE NEED COFFEE TO WAKE UP EVERY MORNING...
© 1985 Tribune Media Services, Inc. All Rights Reserved
BUT I HAVE SOMETHING MUCH MORE EFFECTIVE...
WREN BREATH.

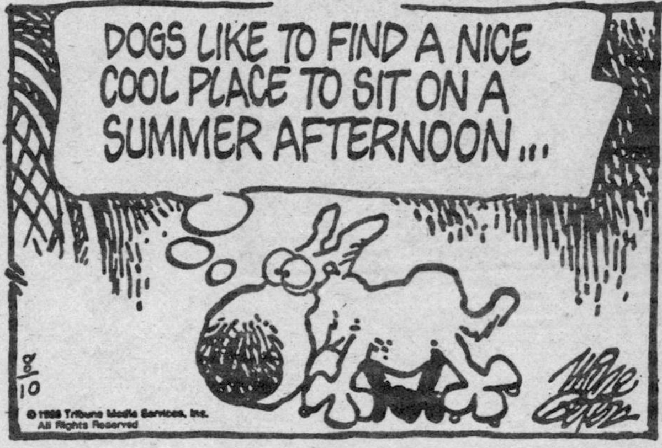
DOGS LIKE TO FIND A NICE COOL PLACE TO SIT ON A SUMMER AFTERNOON...
8/10
© Tribune Media Services, Inc.
All Rights Reserved

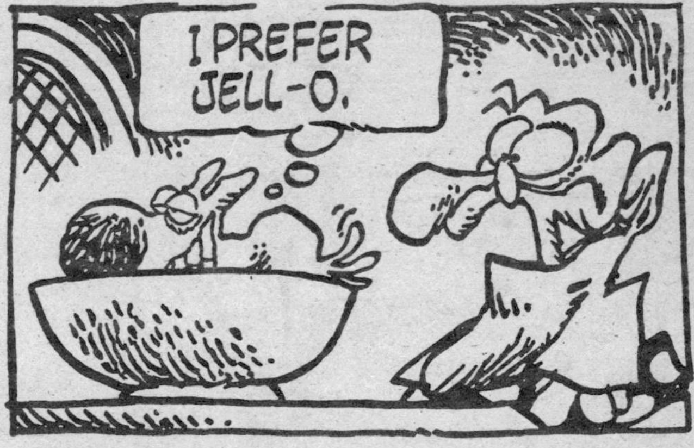
I PREFER JELL-O.

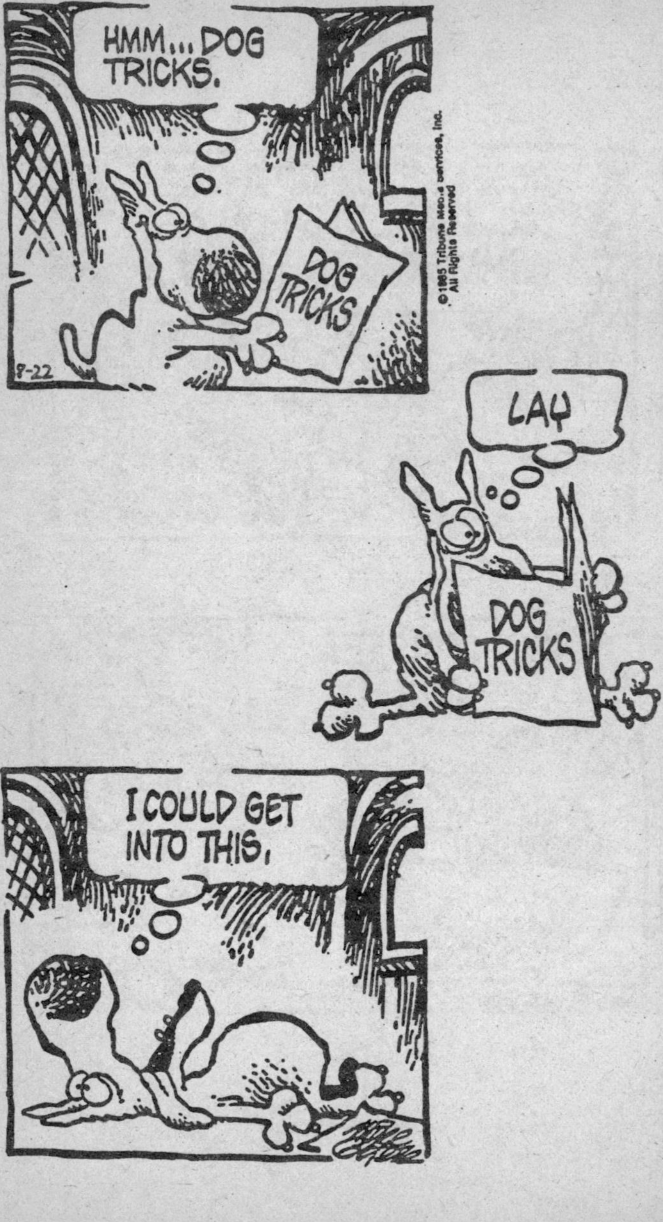
HMM... DOG TRICKS.
DOG TRICKS
8-22
© 1985 Tribune Media Services, Inc. All Rights Reserved
LAY
DOG TRICKS
I COULD GET INTO THIS.

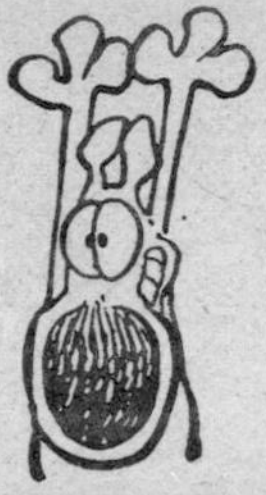

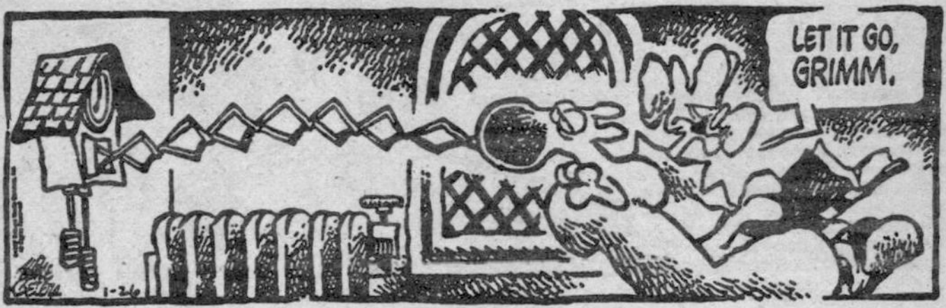
LET IT GO, GRIMM.
1-26

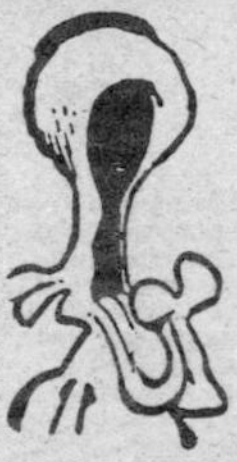

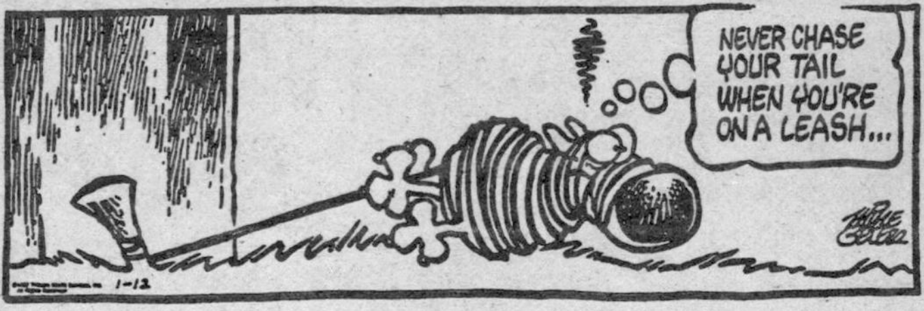
NEVER CHASE YOUR TAIL WHEN YOU'RE ON A LEASH...
1-12

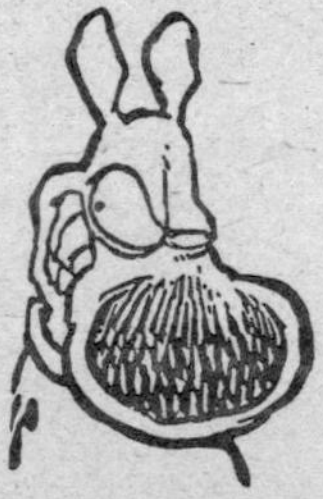

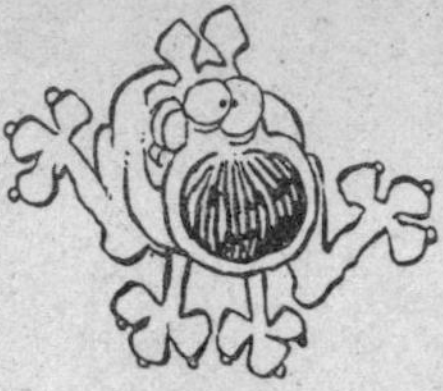

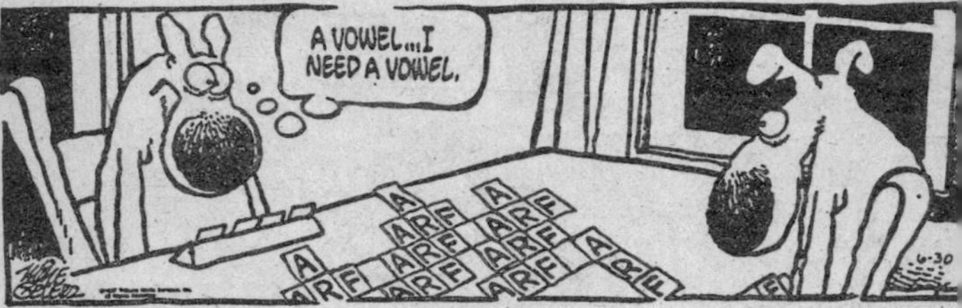
A VOWEL...I NEED A VOWEL.

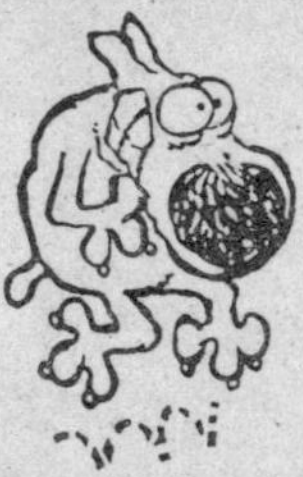

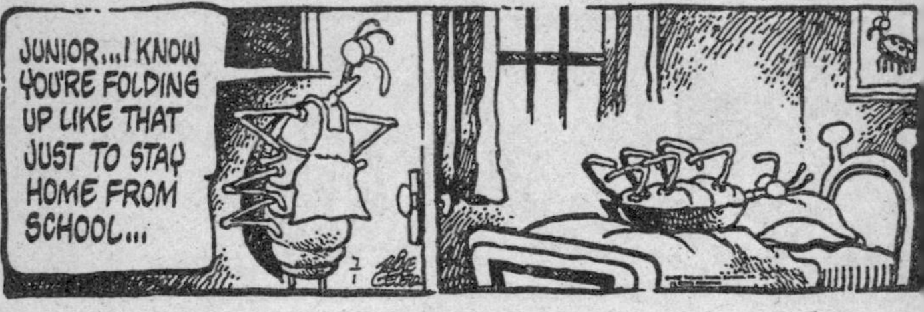
JUNIOR...I KNOW YOU'RE FOLDING UP LIKE THAT JUST TO STAY HOME FROM SCHOOL...

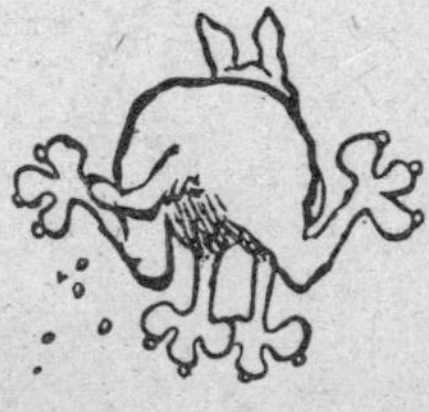

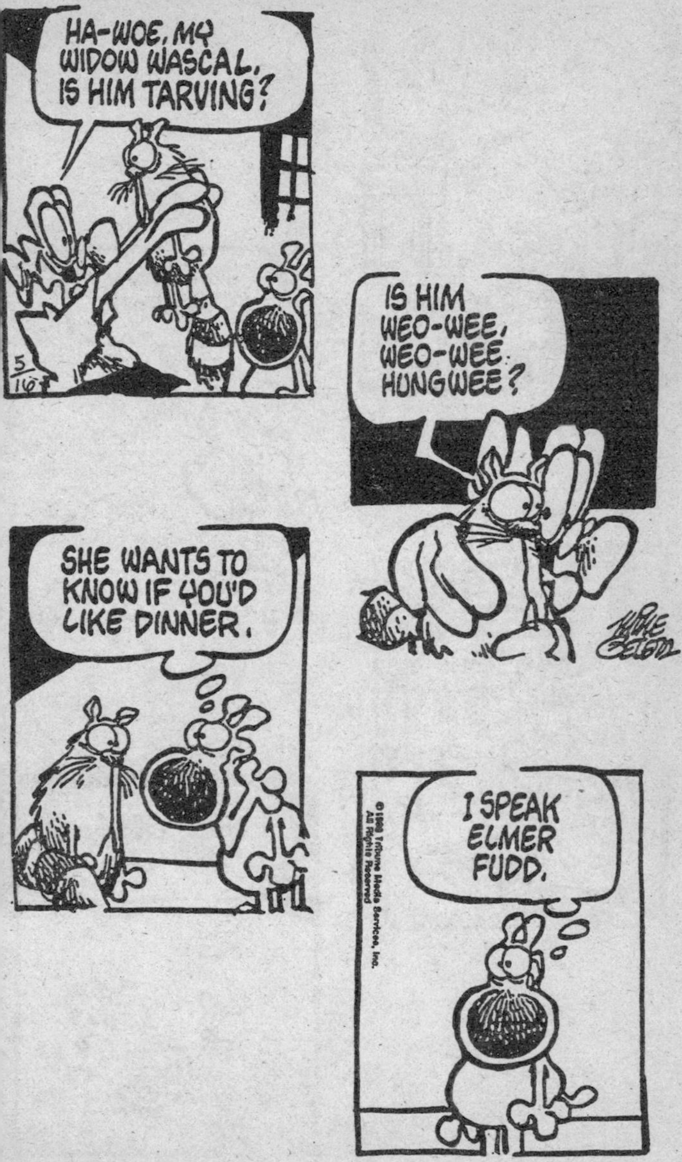
HA-WOE, MY WIDOW WASCAL, IS HIM TARVING?
5/16
IS HIM WEO-WEE, WEO-WEE HUNGWEE?
SHE WANTS TO KNOW IF YOU'D LIKE DINNER.
I SPEAK ELMER FUDD.

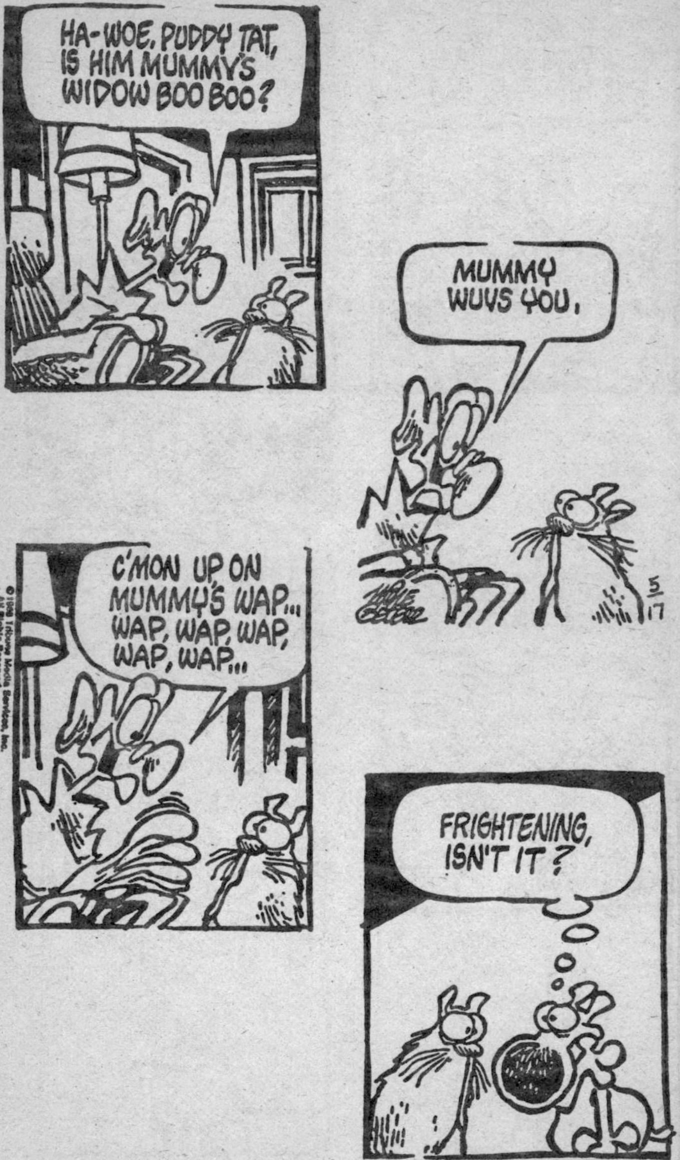
HA-WOE, PUDDY TAT, IS HIM MUMMY'S WIDOW BOO BOO?
C'MON UP ON MUMMY'S WAP... WAP, WAP, WAP, WAP, WAP...
MUMMY WUVS YOU.
5/17
FRIGHTENING, ISN'T IT?

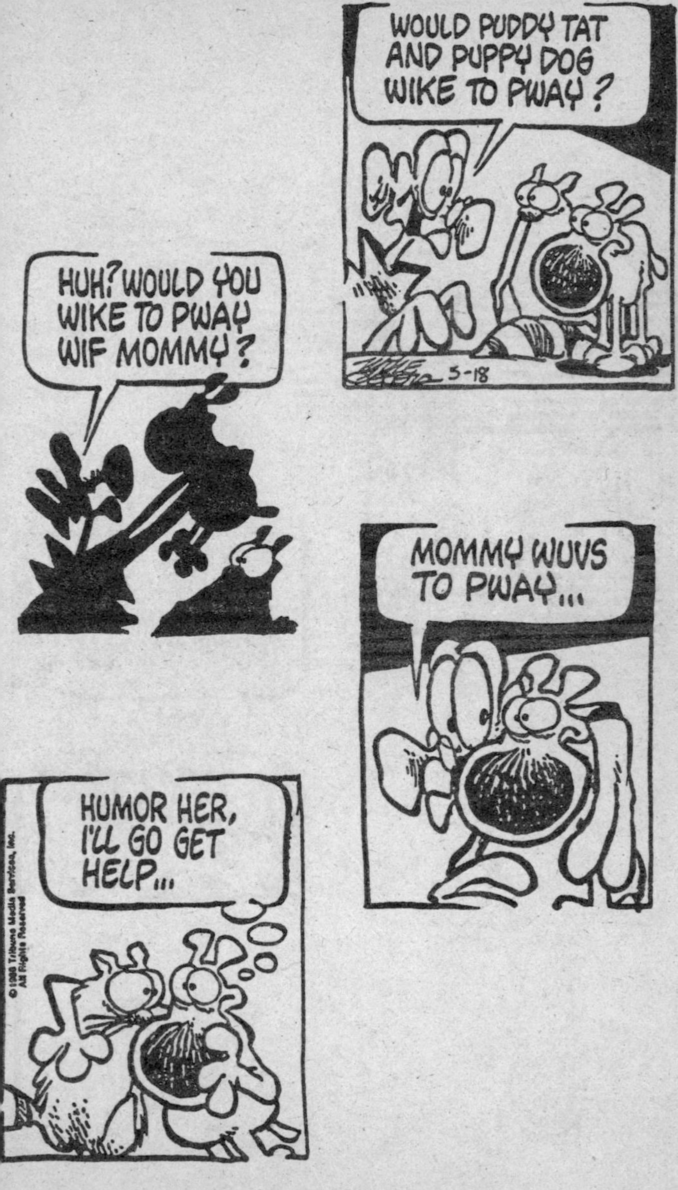

© 1988 Tribune Media Services, Inc.
All Rights Reserved
HUMOR HER, I'LL GO GET HELP...
HUH? WOULD YOU WIKE TO PWAY WIF MOMMY?
MOMMY WUVS TO PWAY...
WOULD PUDDY TAT AND PUPPY DOG WIKE TO PWAY?
5-18

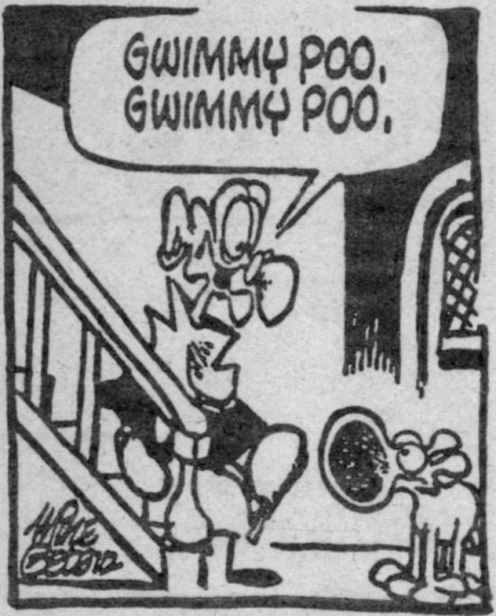
GWIMMY POO,
GWIMMY POO.

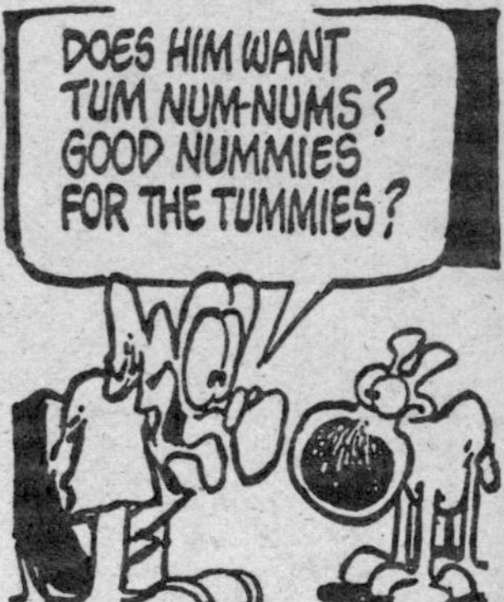
DOES HIM WANT TUM NUM-NUMS? GOOD NUMMIES FOR THE TUMMIES?

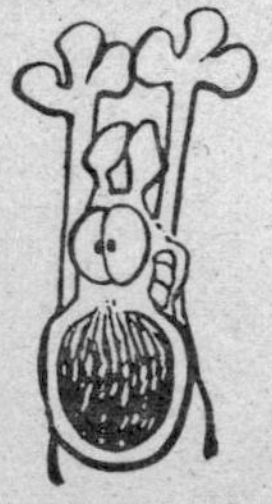

5-19

© 1988 Tribune Media Services, Inc.
All Rights Reserved

THE LEGS
GO NEXT.

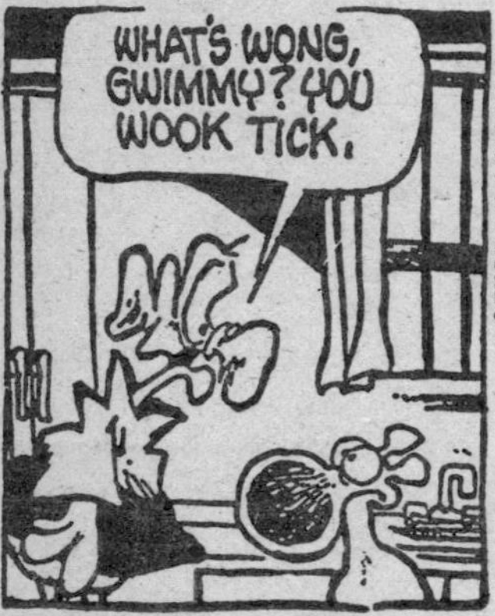
WHAT'S WONG, GWIMMY? YOU WOOK TICK.

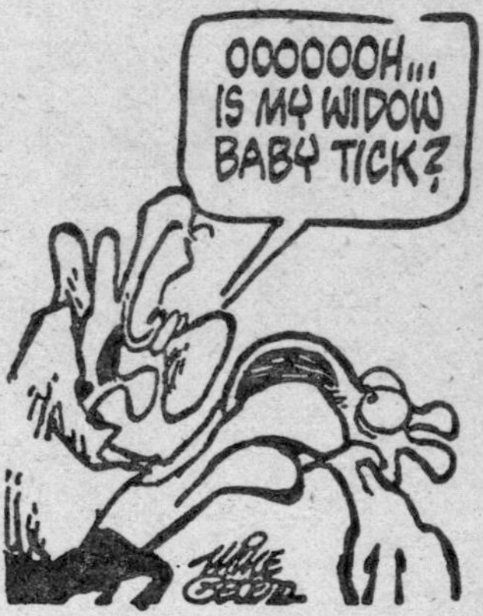
OOOOOOH... IS MY WIDOW BABY TICK?

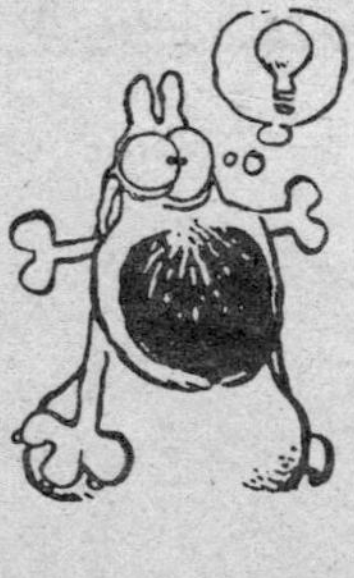

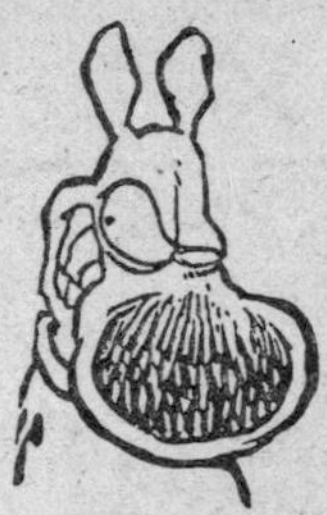

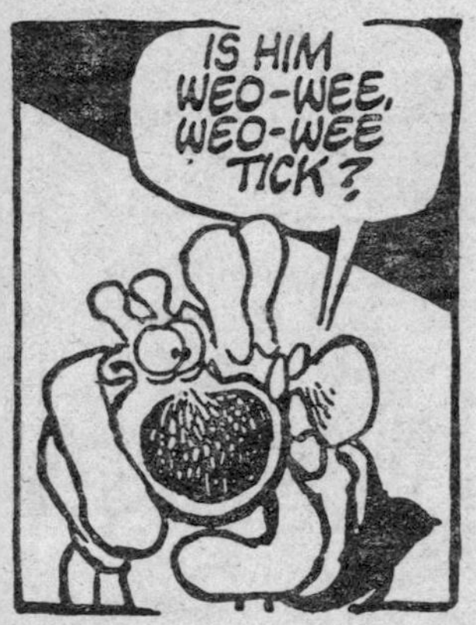
IS HIM WEO-WEE, WEO-WEE TICK?

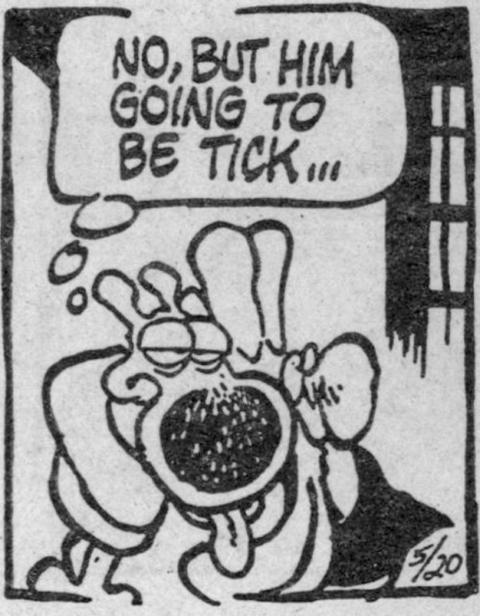
NO, BUT HIM GOING TO BE TICK...
5/20

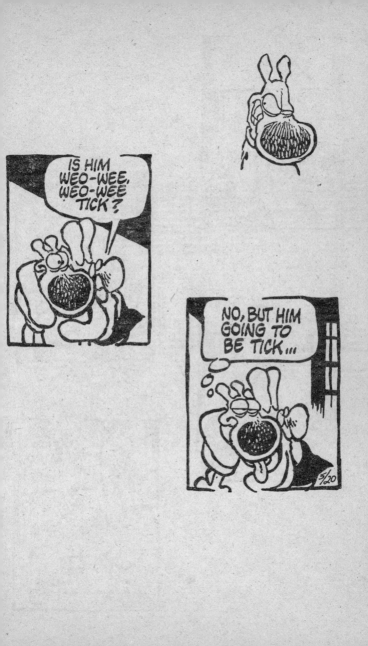

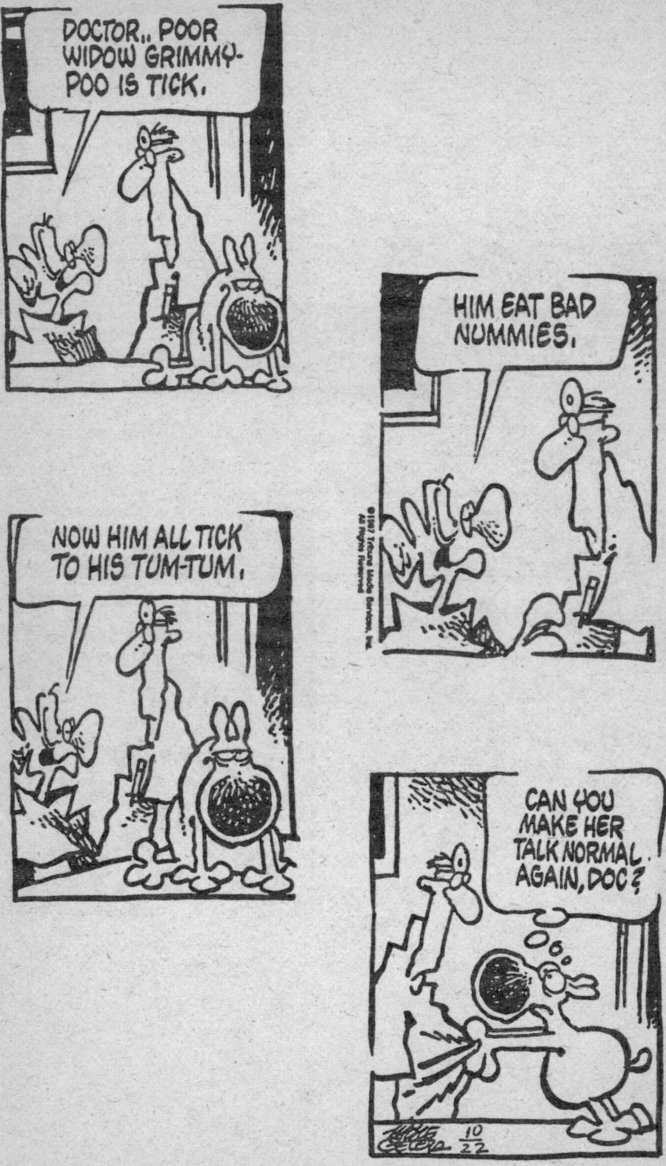
DOCTOR.. POOR WIDOW GRIMMY-POO IS TICK.
HIM EAT BAD NUMMIES.
NOW HIM ALL TICK TO HIS TUM-TUM.
CAN YOU MAKE HER TALK NORMAL AGAIN, DOC?
©1987 Tribune Media Services, Inc. All Rights Reserved
10/22

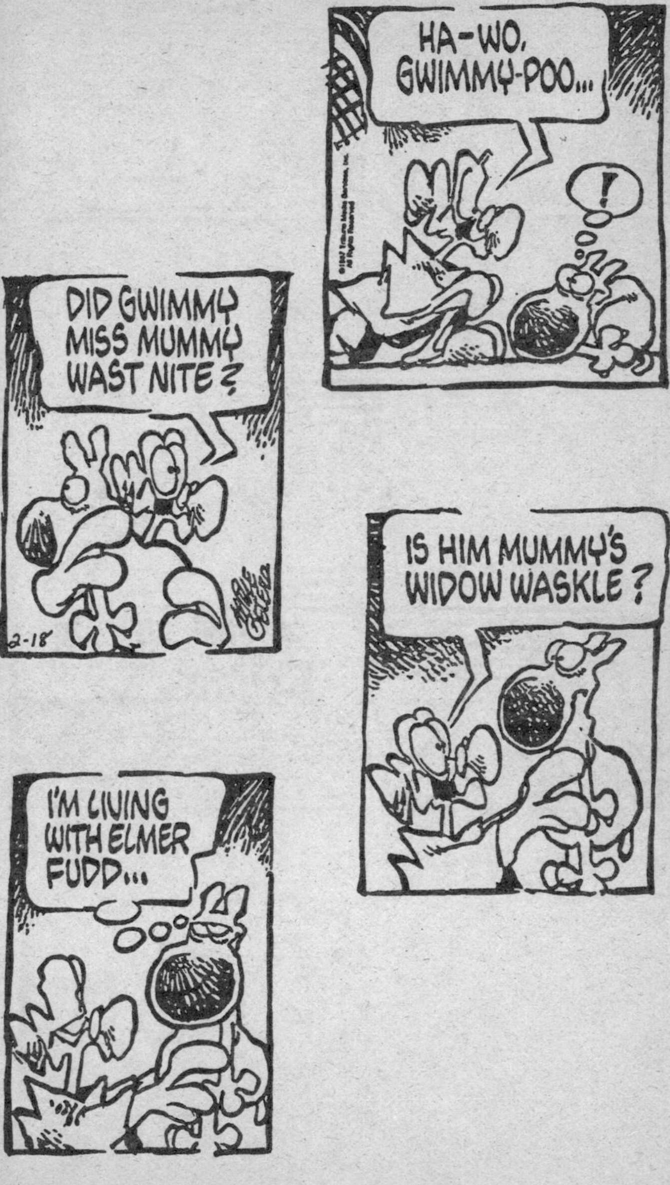
HA-WO, GWIMMY-POO...
!
DID GWIMMY MISS MUMMY WAST NITE?
2-18
IS HIM MUMMY'S WIDOW WASKLE?
I'M LIVING WITH ELMER FUDD...

I LOVE WHEN MY FLEAS THROW ME A SURPRISE PARTY...

HE FELL FOR THE OLD CATNIP IN THE COPIER TRICK,

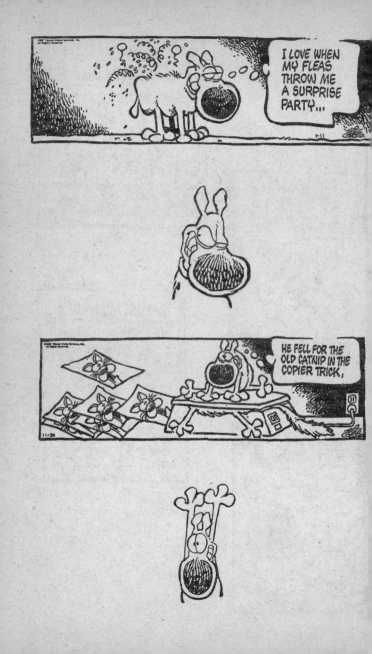

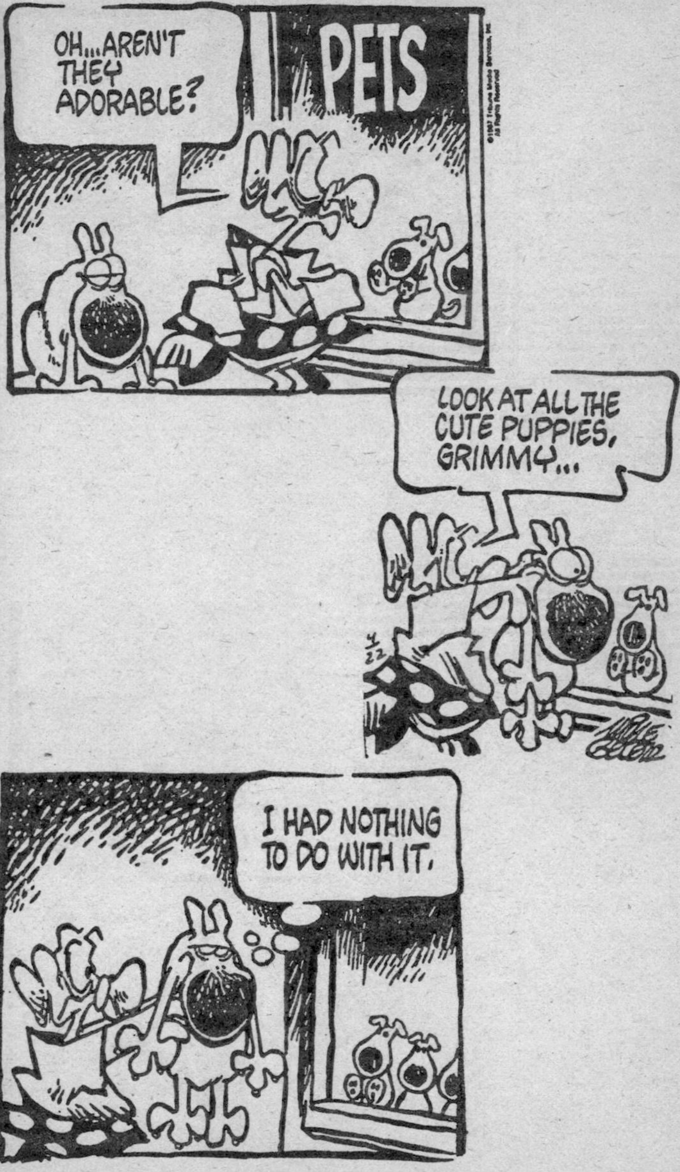
OH...AREN'T THEY ADORABLE?
PETS
LOOK AT ALL THE CUTE PUPPIES, GRIMMY...
4/22
I HAD NOTHING TO DO WITH IT.

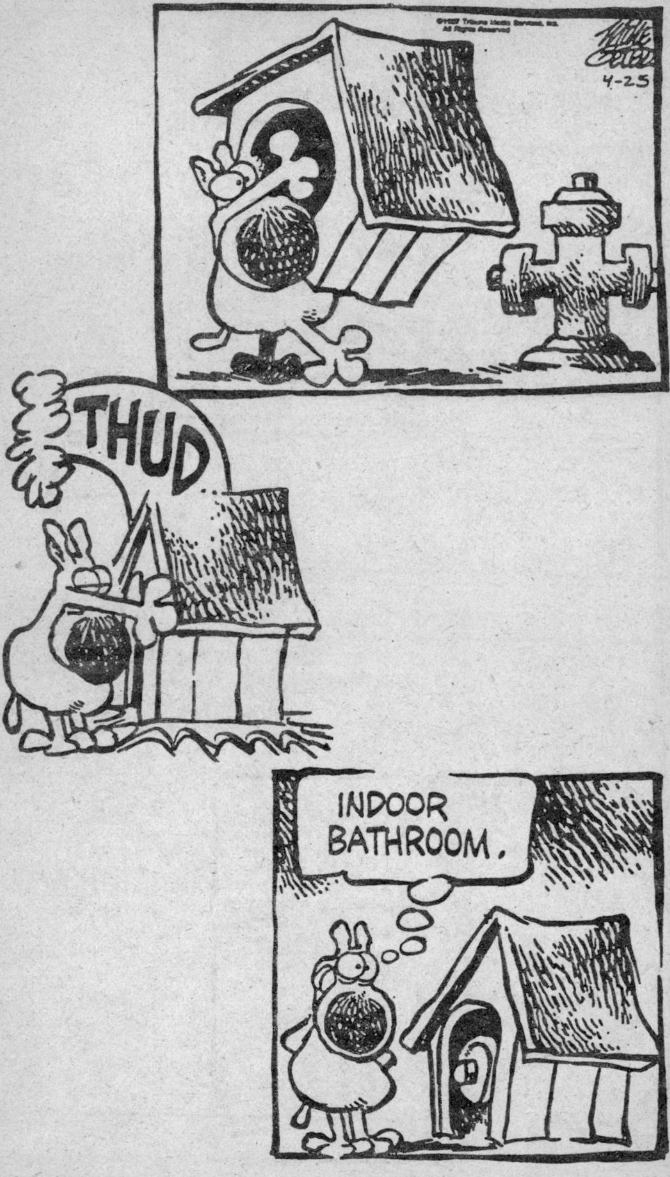

4-25
THUD
INDOOR BATHROOM.

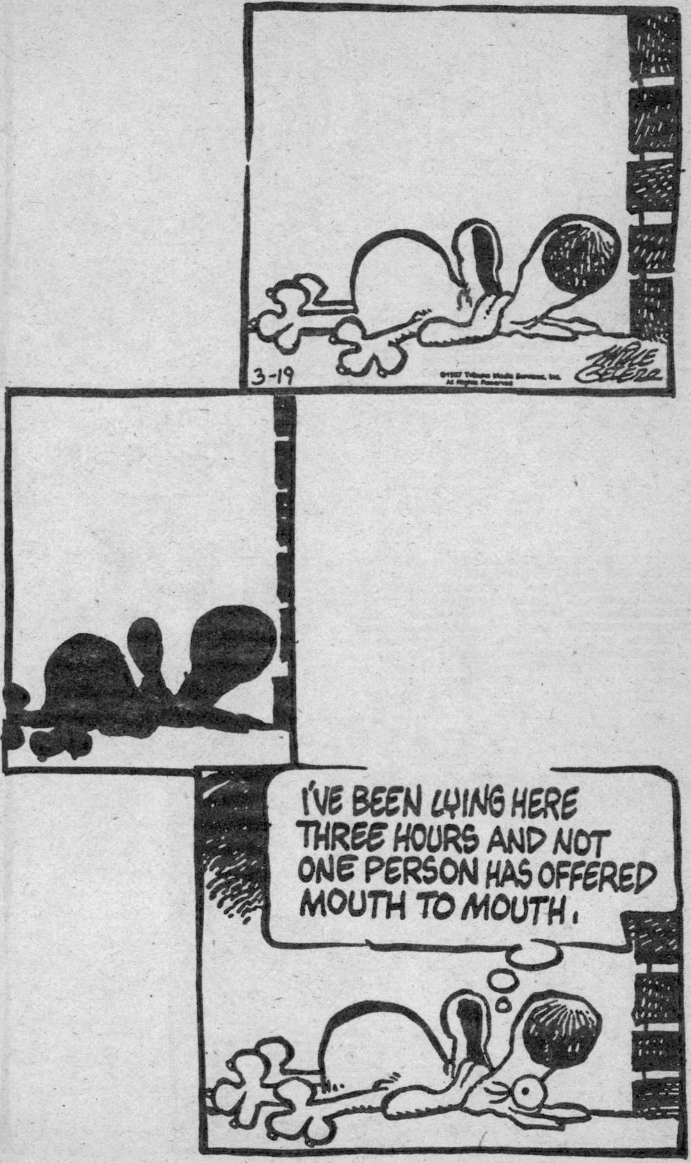
3-19
I'VE BEEN LYING HERE THREE HOURS AND NOT ONE PERSON HAS OFFERED MOUTH TO MOUTH.

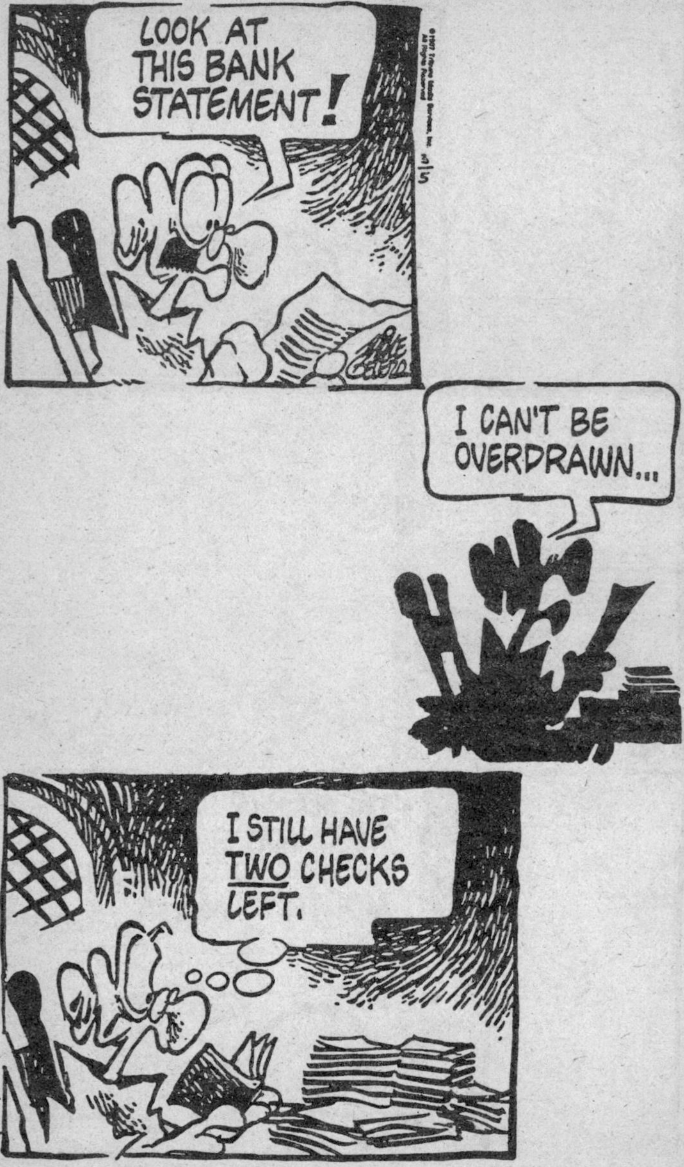
LOOK AT THIS BANK STATEMENT!
I CAN'T BE OVERDRAWN...
I STILL HAVE TWO CHECKS LEFT.

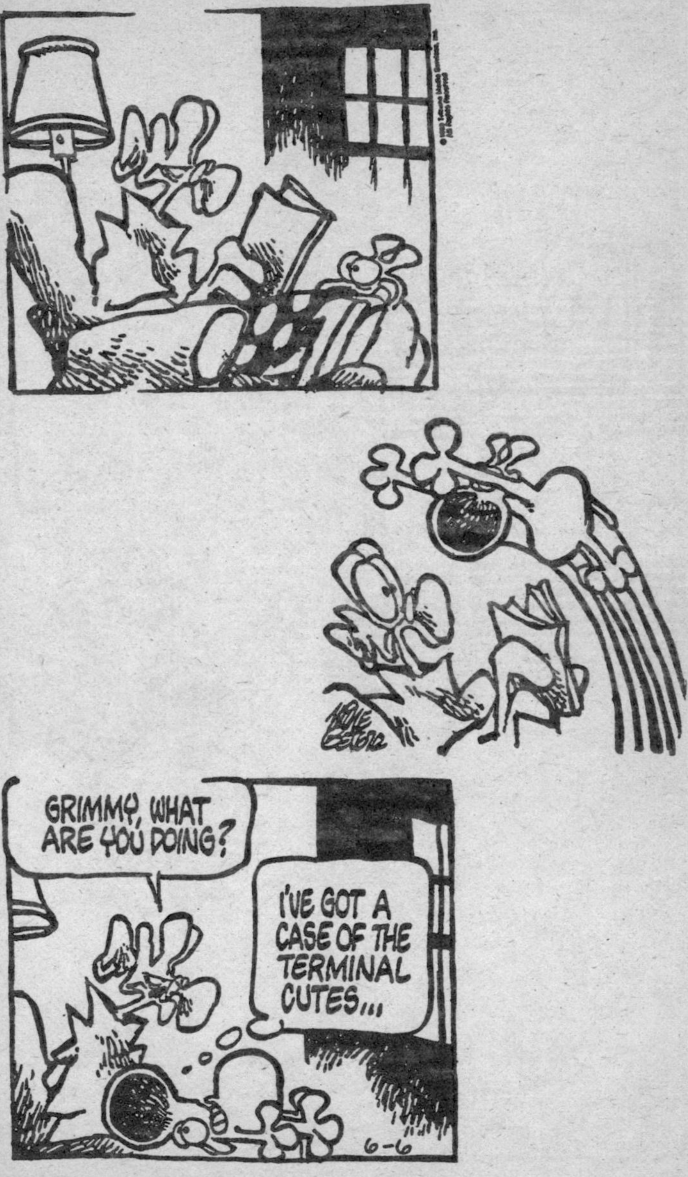
GRIMMY, WHAT ARE YOU DOING?
I'VE GOT A CASE OF THE TERMINAL CUTES...
6-6

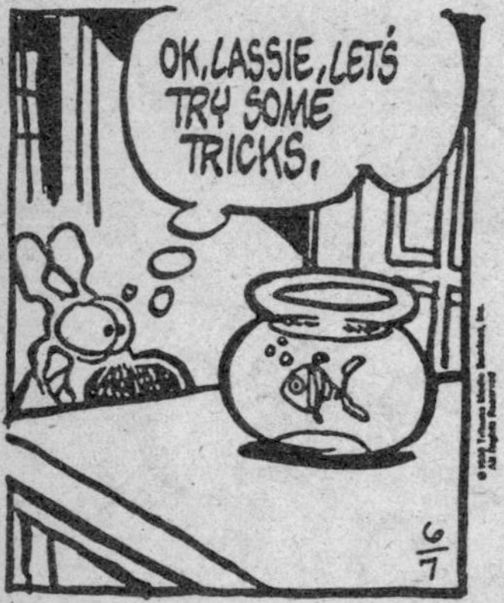
OK, LASSIE, LET'S TRY SOME TRICKS.
6/7

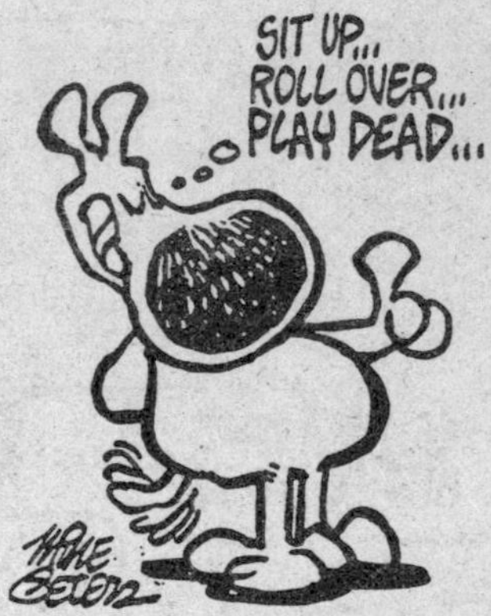
SIT UP... ROLL OVER... PLAY DEAD...
MIKE PETERS

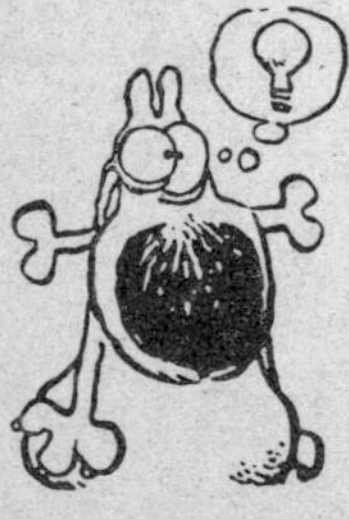

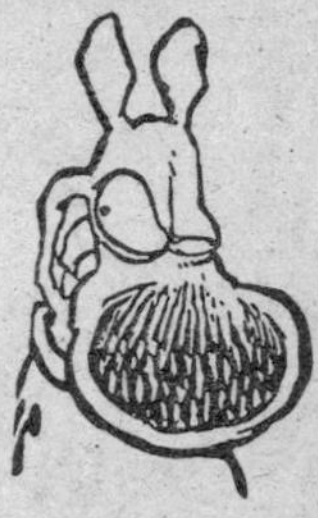

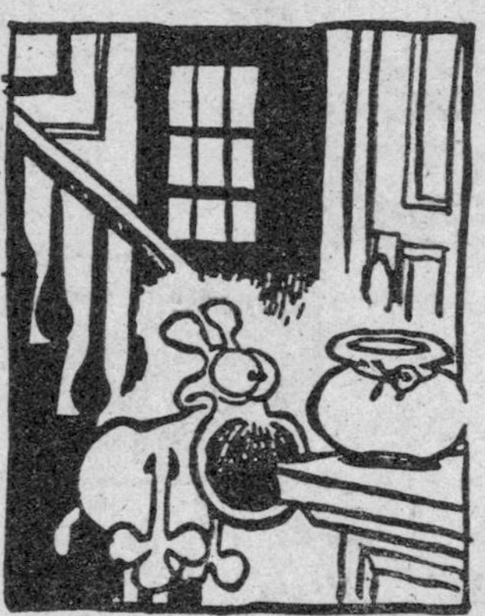

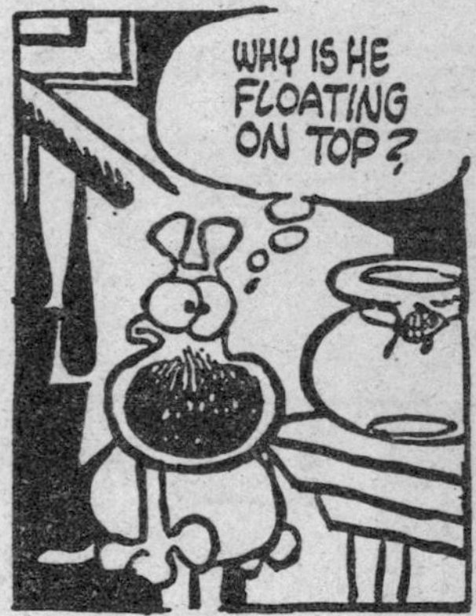
WHY IS HE FLOATING ON TOP?

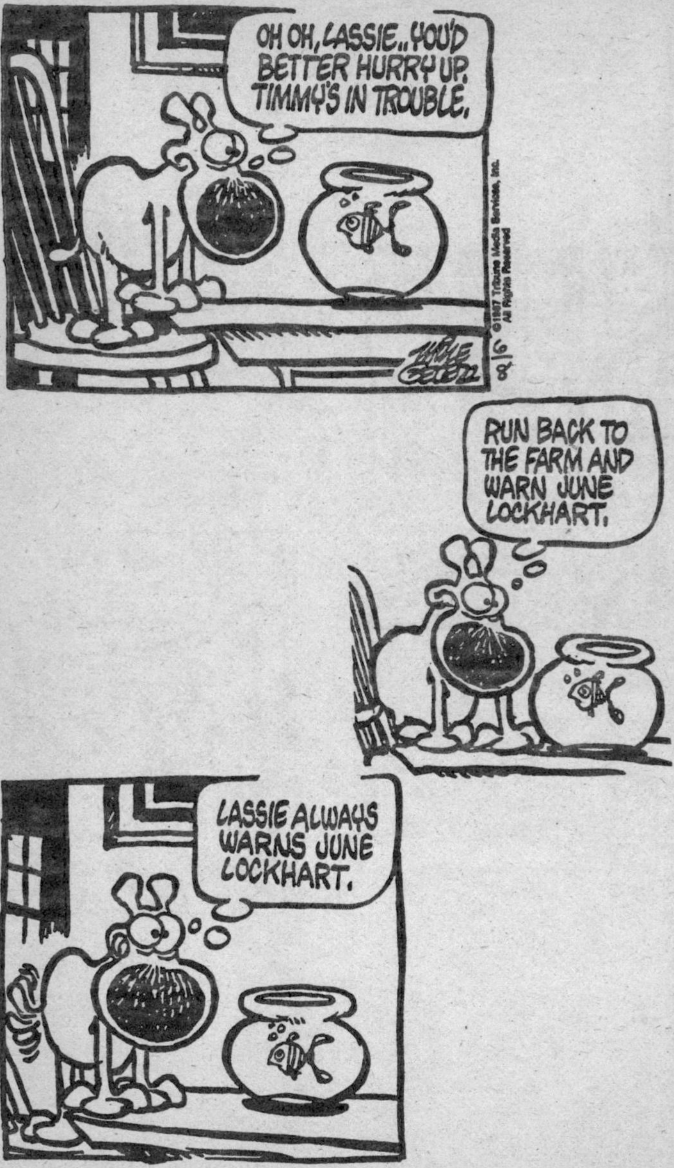
OH OH, LASSIE.. YOU'D BETTER HURRY UP. TIMMY'S IN TROUBLE.
©1987 Tribune Media Services, Inc. All Rights Reserved
RUN BACK TO THE FARM AND WARN JUNE LOCKHART.
LASSIE ALWAYS WARNS JUNE LOCKHART.

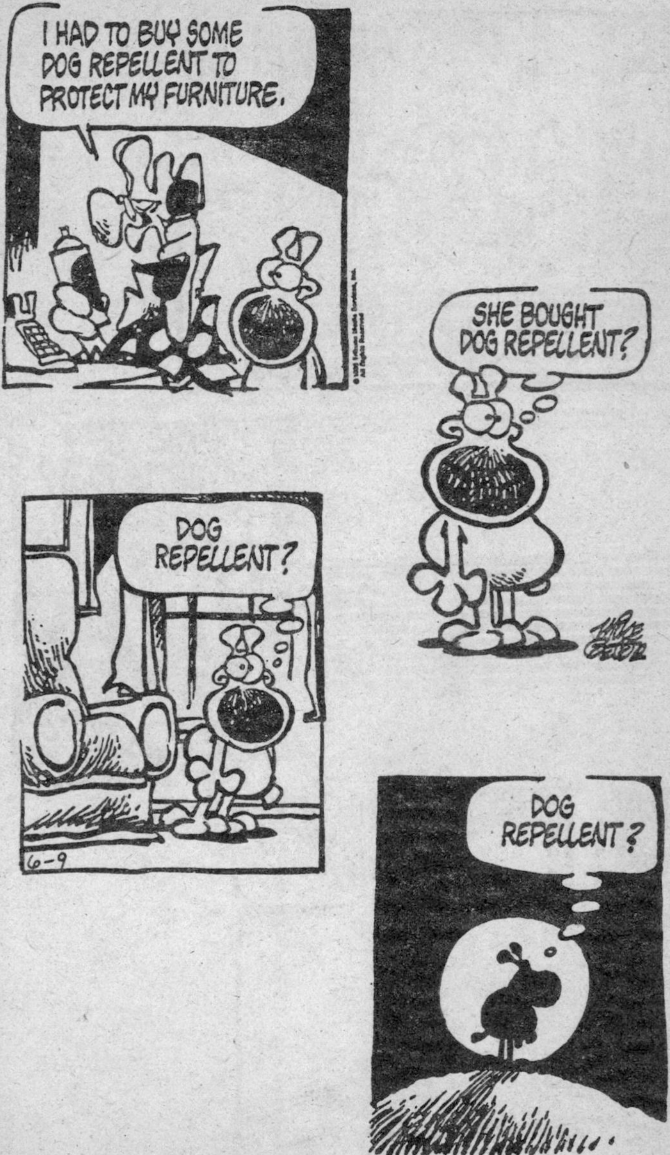
I HAD TO BUY SOME DOG REPELLENT TO PROTECT MY FURNITURE.
DOG REPELLENT?
6-9
SHE BOUGHT DOG REPELLENT?
DOG REPELLENT?

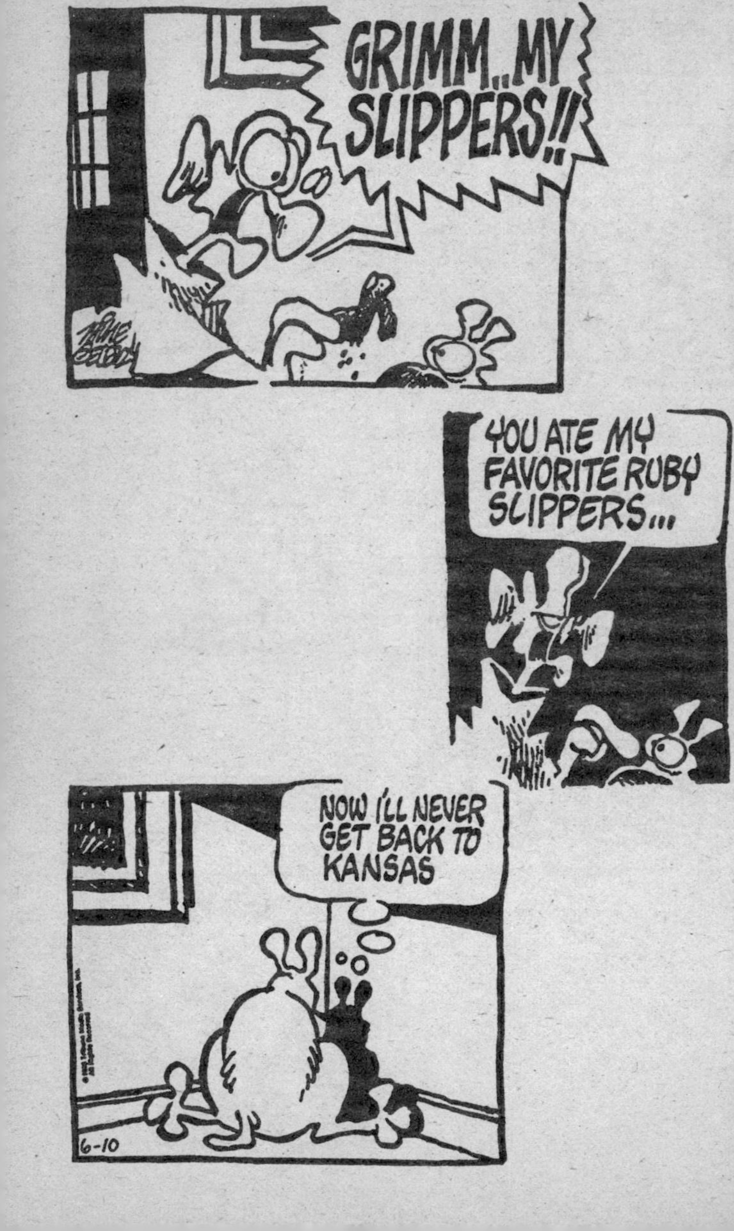
GRIMM...MY SLIPPERS!!
YOU ATE MY FAVORITE RUBY SLIPPERS...
NOW I'LL NEVER GET BACK TO KANSAS
6-10

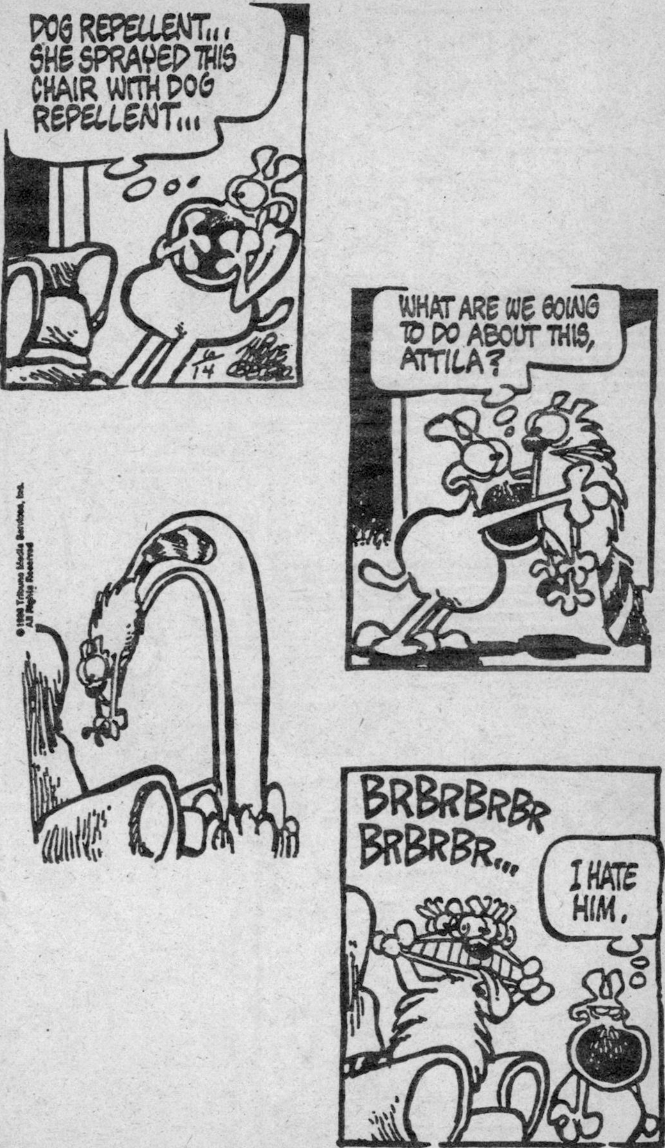
DOG REPELLENT... SHE SPRAYED THIS CHAIR WITH DOG REPELLENT...
WHAT ARE WE GOING TO DO ABOUT THIS, ATTILA?
Tribune Media Services, Inc.
All Rights Reserved
BRBRBRBR BRBRBR...
I HATE HIM.

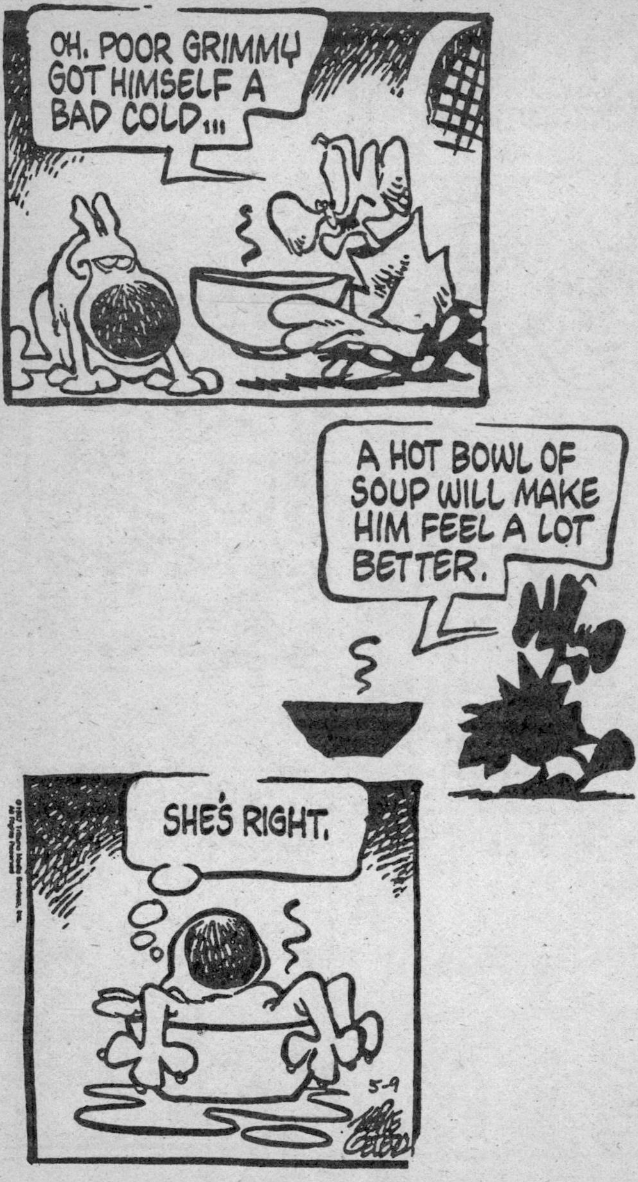
OH. POOR GRIMMY GOT HIMSELF A BAD COLD...
A HOT BOWL OF SOUP WILL MAKE HIM FEEL A LOT BETTER.
SHE'S RIGHT.
5-9

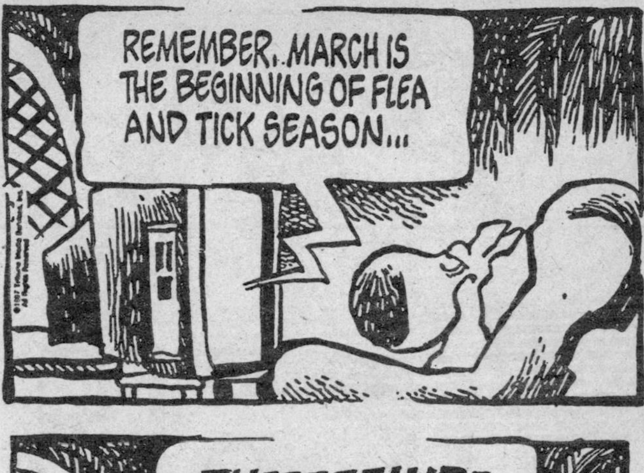
REMEMBER..MARCH IS THE BEGINNING OF FLEA AND TICK SEASON...
THEEEEEY'REE BAAAAACK.
3-17

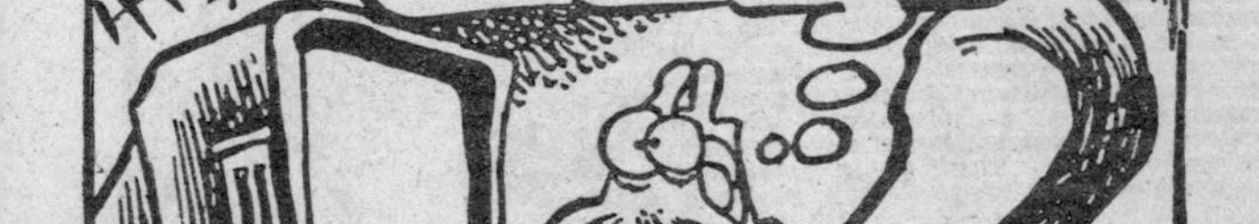
HE FOUND SOME JUNK BONDS.
12-17

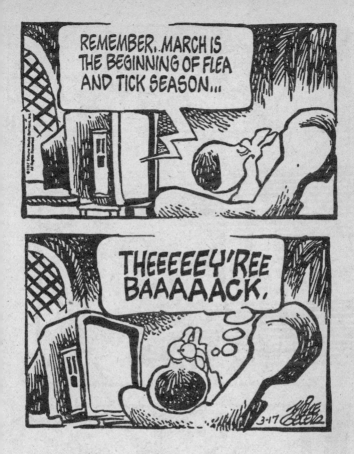

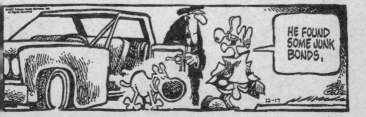

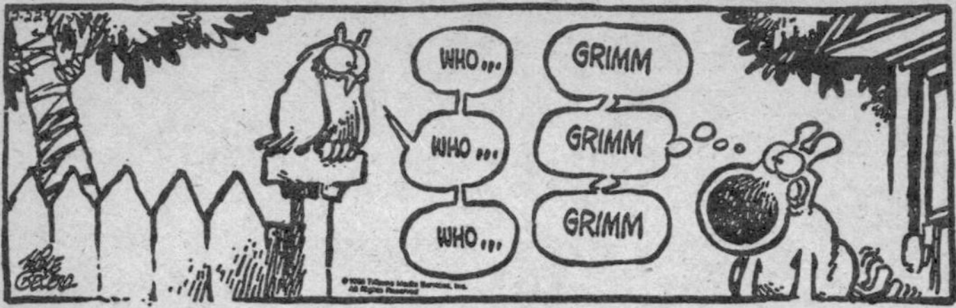
WHO...
WHO...
WHO...
GRIMM
GRIMM
GRIMM

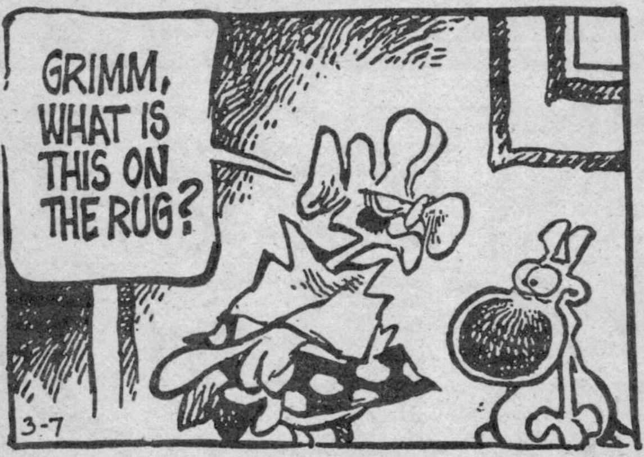
GRIMM, WHAT IS THIS ON THE RUG?
3-7

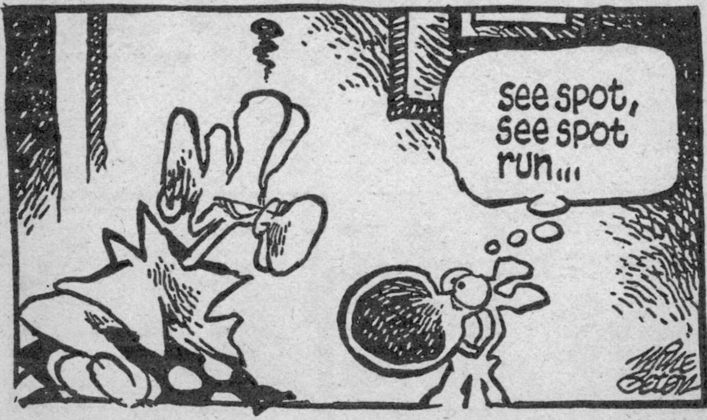
see spot, see spot run...

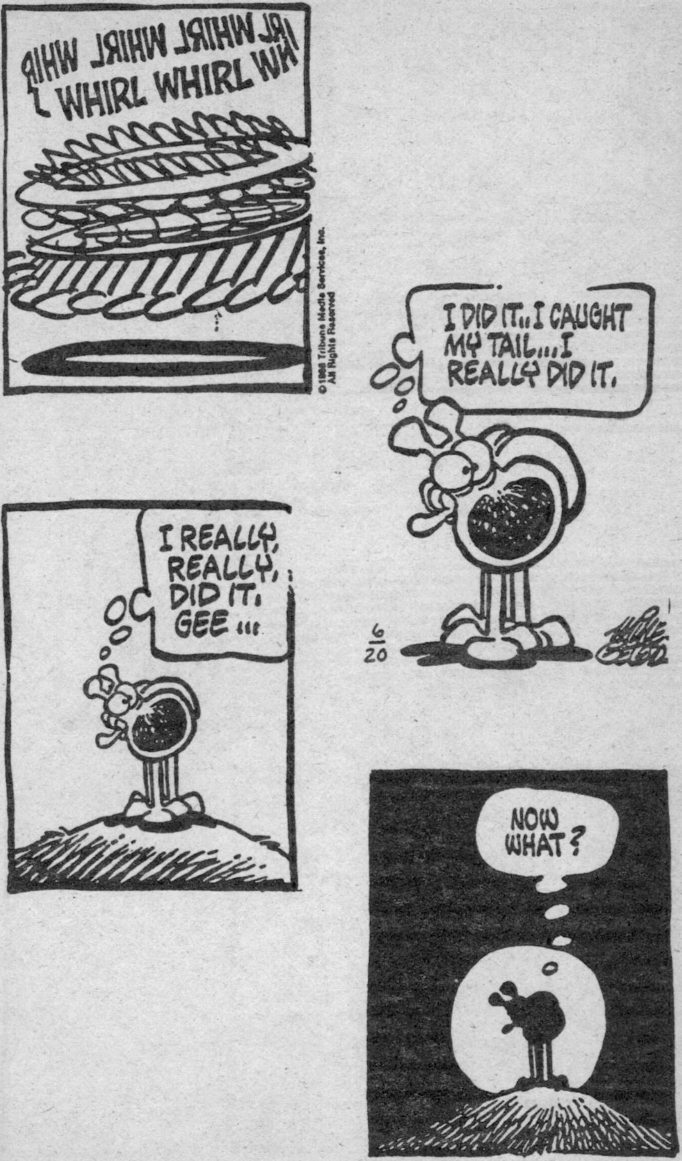

WHIRL WHIRL WHIR
WHIRL WHIRL WH
I DID IT.. I CAUGHT MY TAIL... I REALLY DID IT.
I REALLY, REALLY, DID IT. GEE ...
6/20
NOW WHAT?

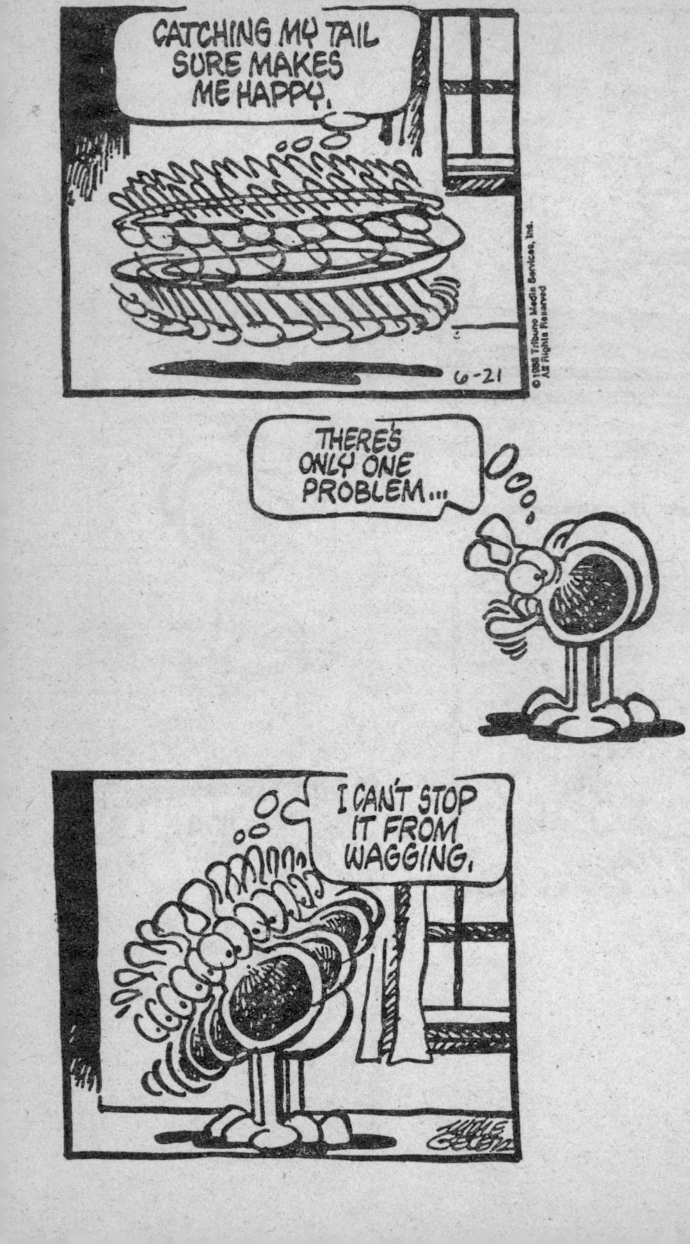
CATCHING MY TAIL SURE MAKES ME HAPPY.
6-21
Tribune Media Services, Inc. All Rights Reserved
THERE'S ONLY ONE PROBLEM...
I CAN'T STOP IT FROM WAGGING.

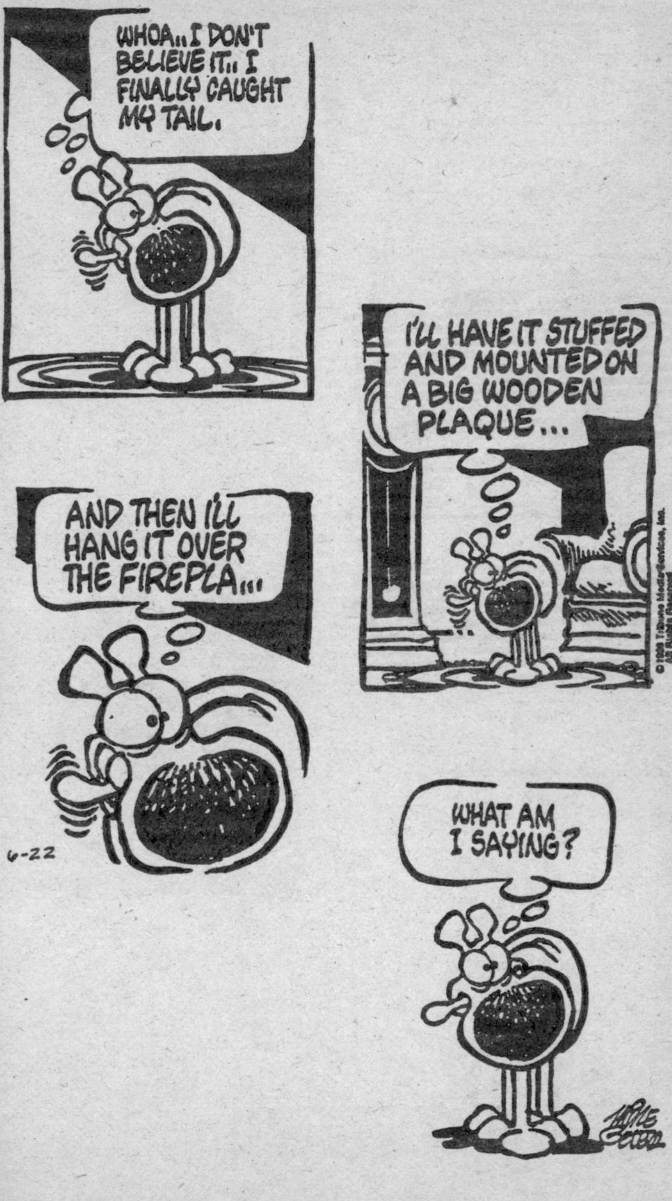
WHOA.. I DON'T BELIEVE IT.. I FINALLY CAUGHT MY TAIL.
I'LL HAVE IT STUFFED AND MOUNTED ON A BIG WOODEN PLAQUE...
AND THEN I'LL HANG IT OVER THE FIREPLA...
6-22
WHAT AM I SAYING?

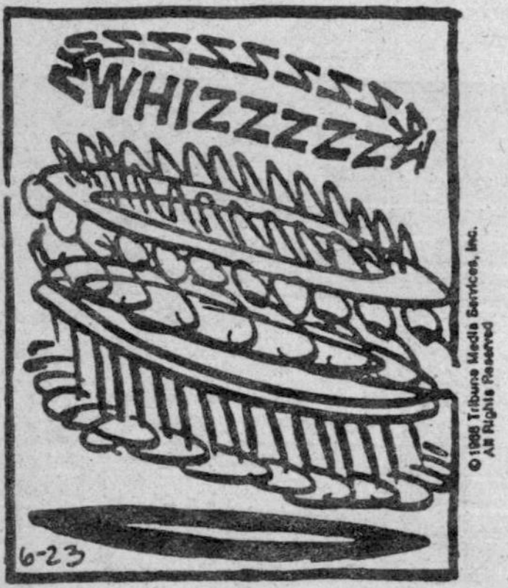
SSSSSSSS
WHIZZZZZZ
6-23
© 1988 Tribune Media Services, Inc.
All Rights Reserved

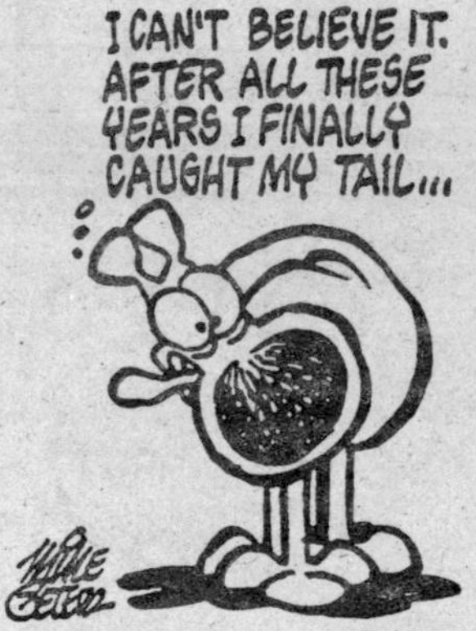
I CAN'T BELIEVE IT. AFTER ALL THESE YEARS I FINALLY CAUGHT MY TAIL...

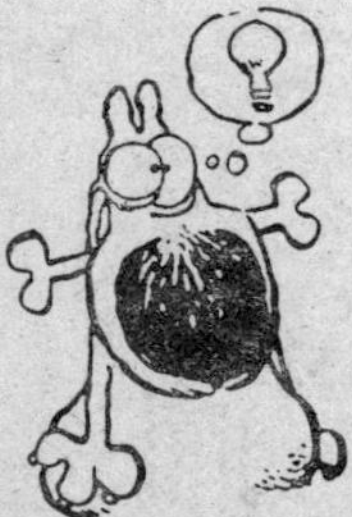

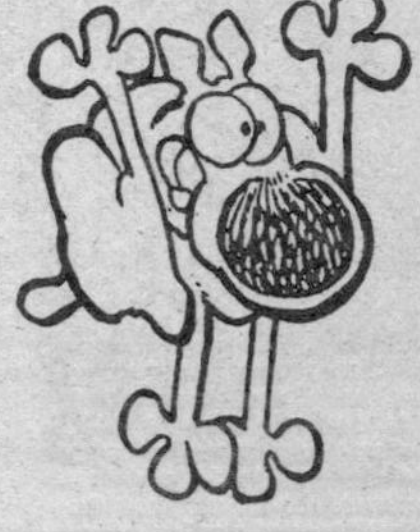

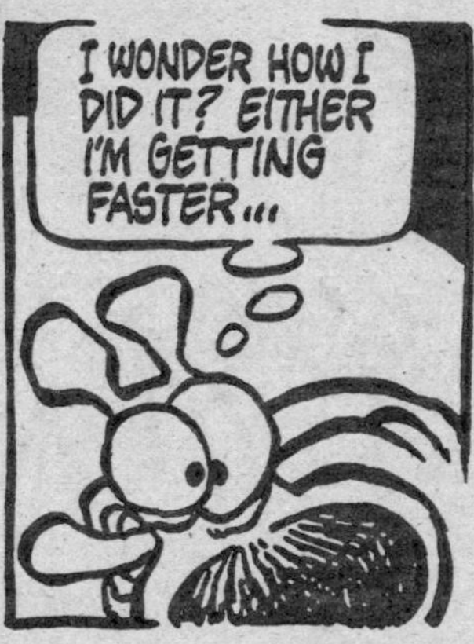
I WONDER HOW I DID IT? EITHER I'M GETTING FASTER...

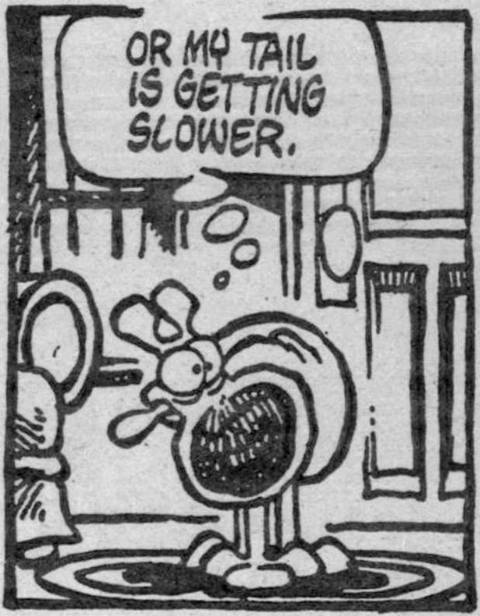
OR MY TAIL IS GETTING SLOWER.

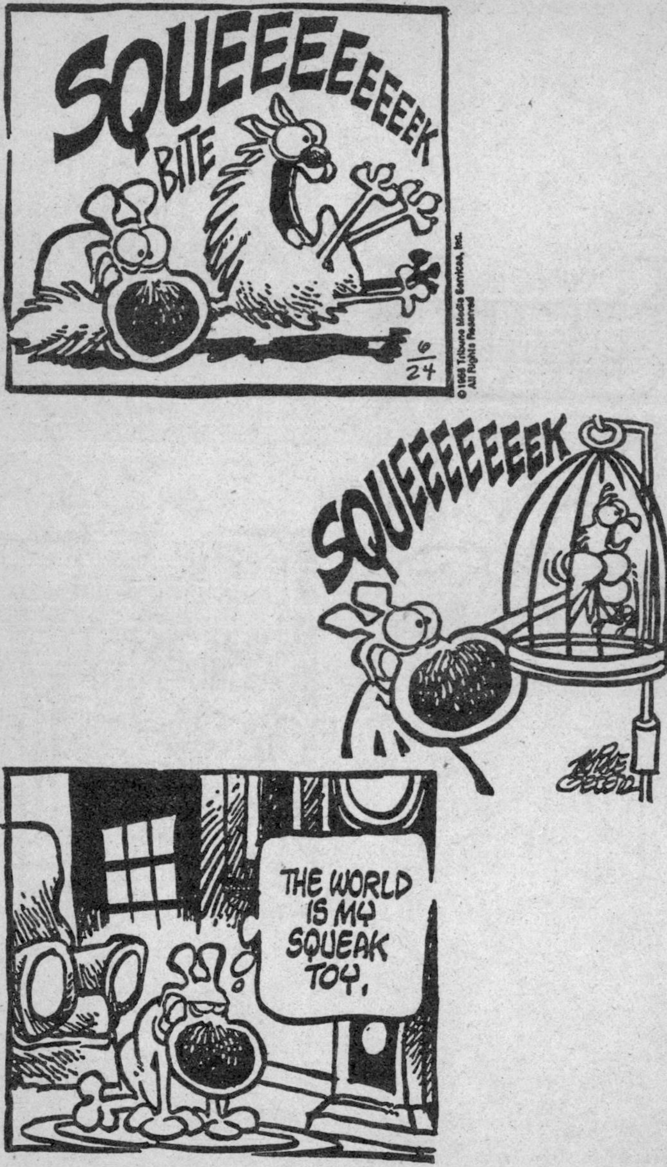
SQUEEEEEEEEK
BITE
SQUEEEEEEEEK
THE WORLD IS MY SQUEAK TOY.

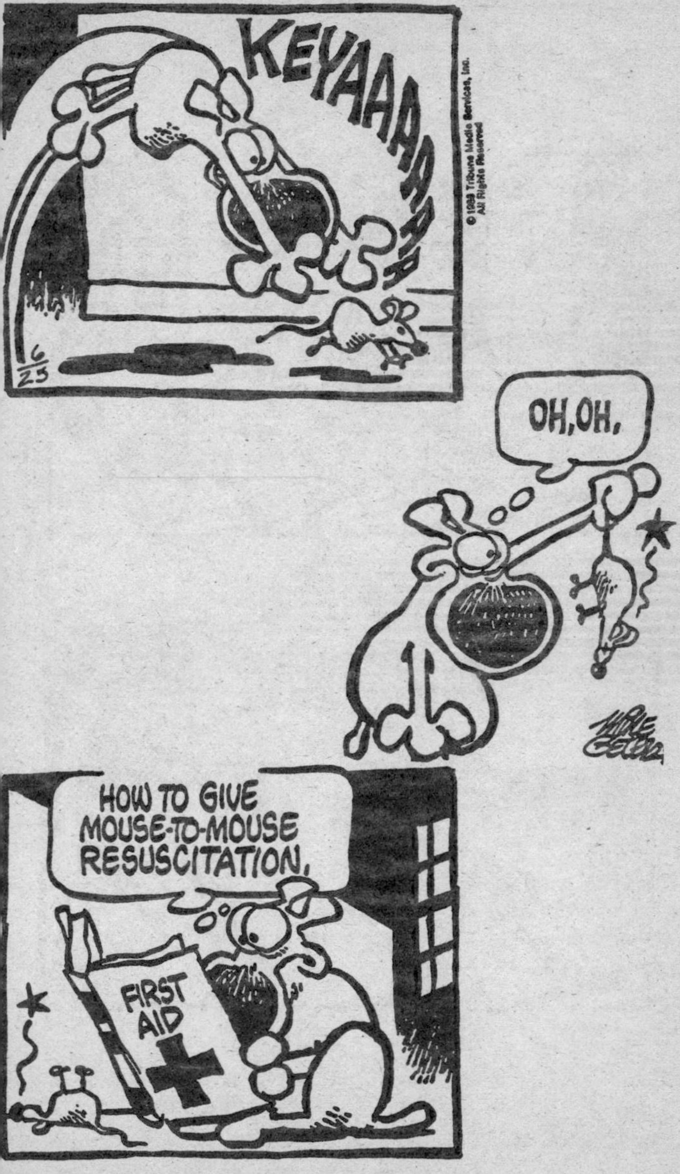
KEYAAAAAAA
6/25
OH, OH.
HOW TO GIVE MOUSE-TO-MOUSE RESUSCITATION.
FIRST AID

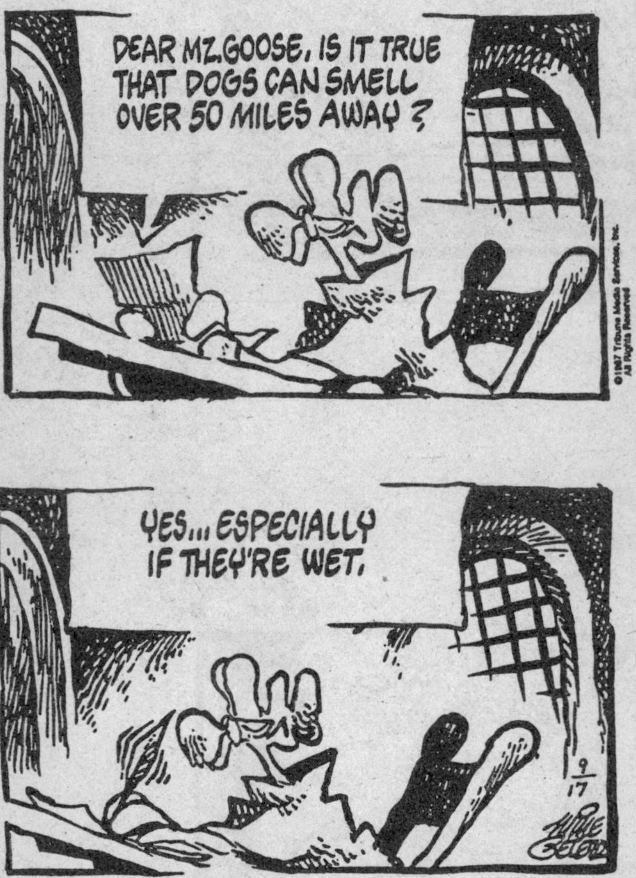
DEAR MZ.GOOSE, IS IT TRUE THAT DOGS CAN SMELL OVER 50 MILES AWAY ?
©1987 Tribune Media Services, Inc. All Rights Reserved
YES... ESPECIALLY IF THEY'RE WET.
9/17

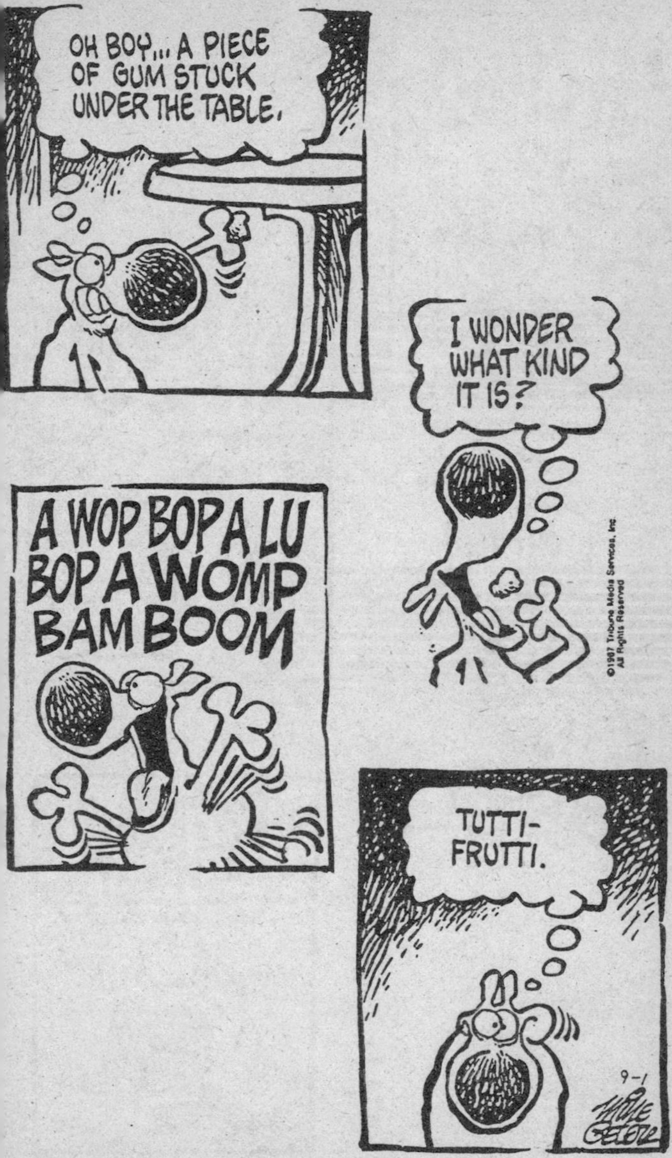
OH BOY... A PIECE OF GUM STUCK UNDER THE TABLE.
I WONDER WHAT KIND IT IS?
A WOP BOP A LU BOP A WOMP BAM BOOM
TUTTI-FRUTTI.
©1987 Tribune Media Services, Inc
All Rights Reserved
9-1

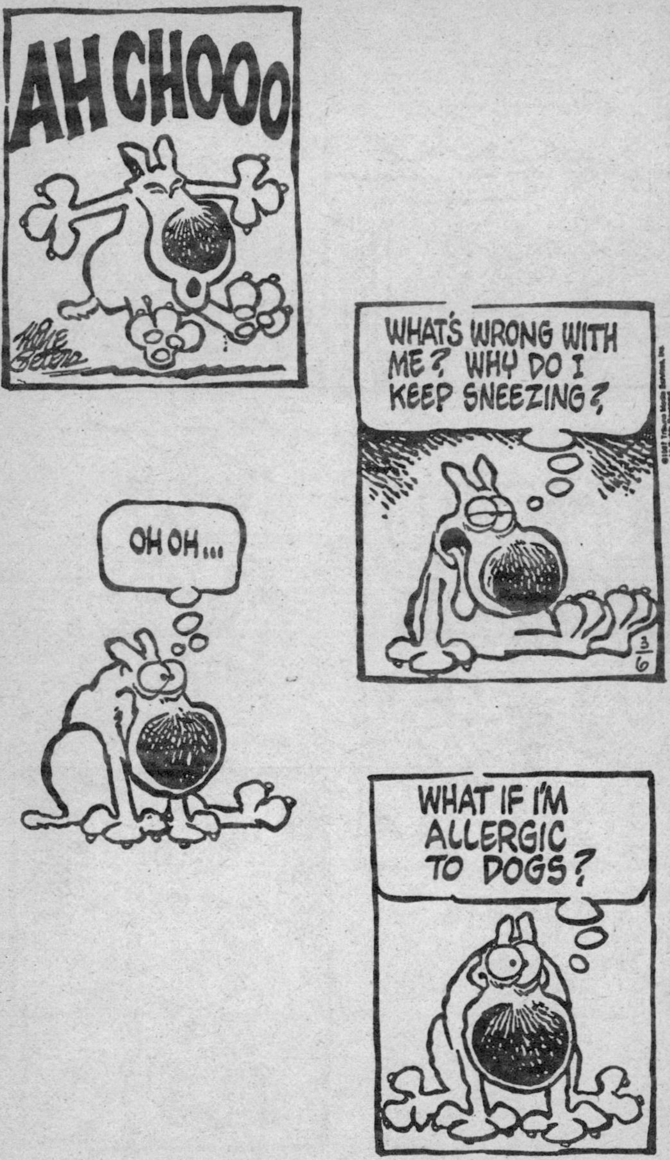
AH CHOOO
WHAT'S WRONG WITH ME? WHY DO I KEEP SNEEZING?
OH OH...
WHAT IF I'M ALLERGIC TO DOGS?
3/6

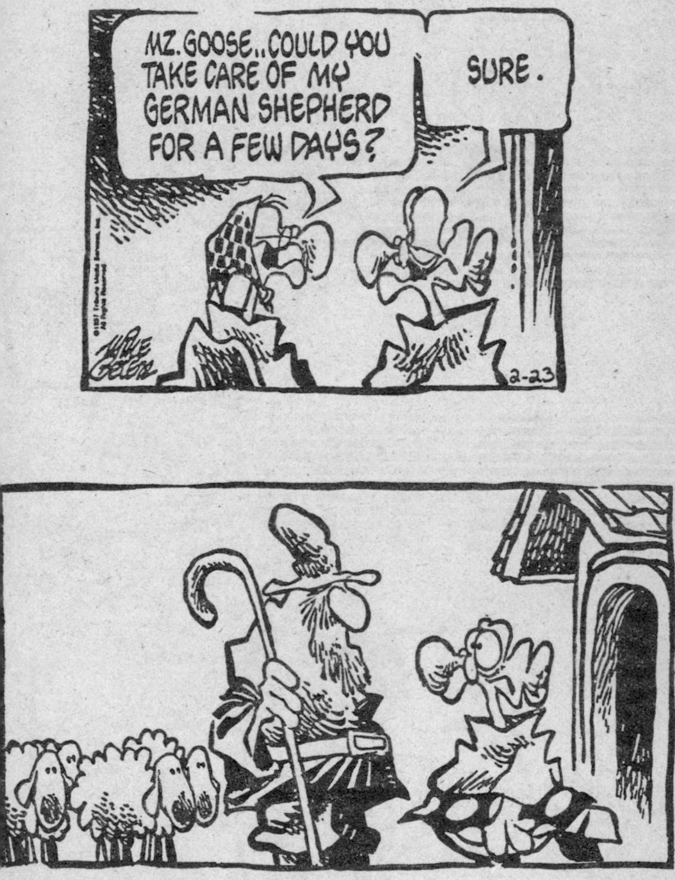
MZ. GOOSE.. COULD YOU TAKE CARE OF MY GERMAN SHEPHERD FOR A FEW DAYS?
SURE.
2-23

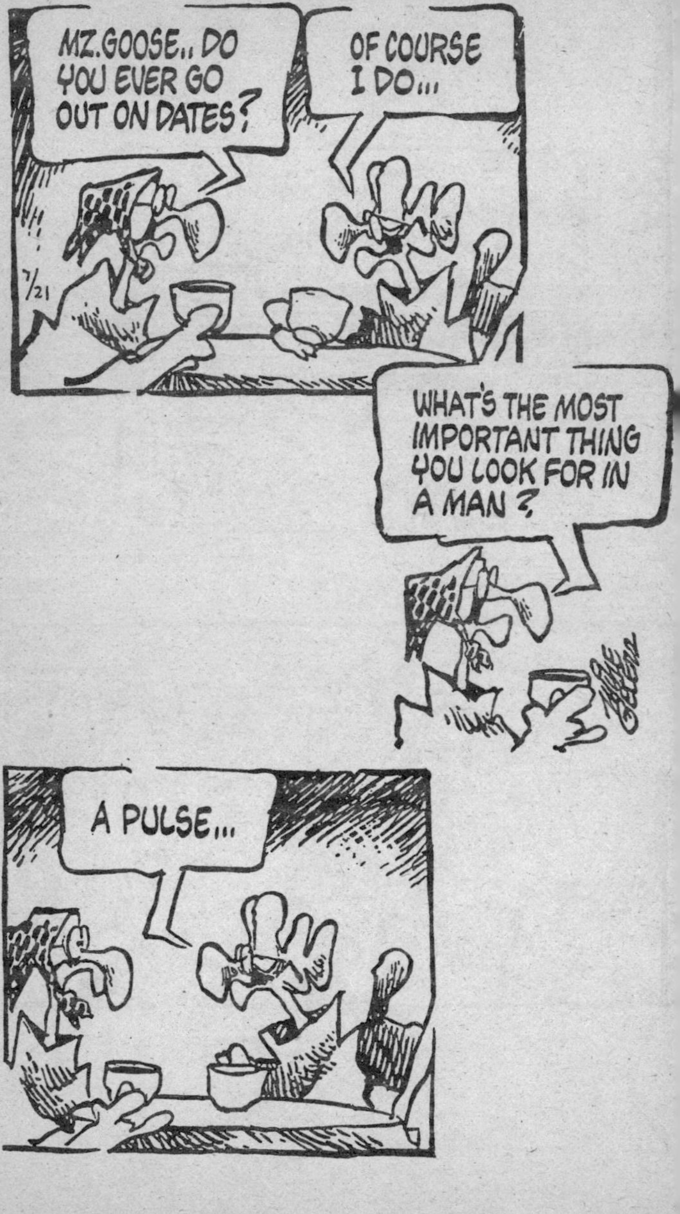
MZ.GOOSE.. DO YOU EVER GO OUT ON DATES?
OF COURSE I DO...
7/21
WHAT'S THE MOST IMPORTANT THING YOU LOOK FOR IN A MAN?
A PULSE...

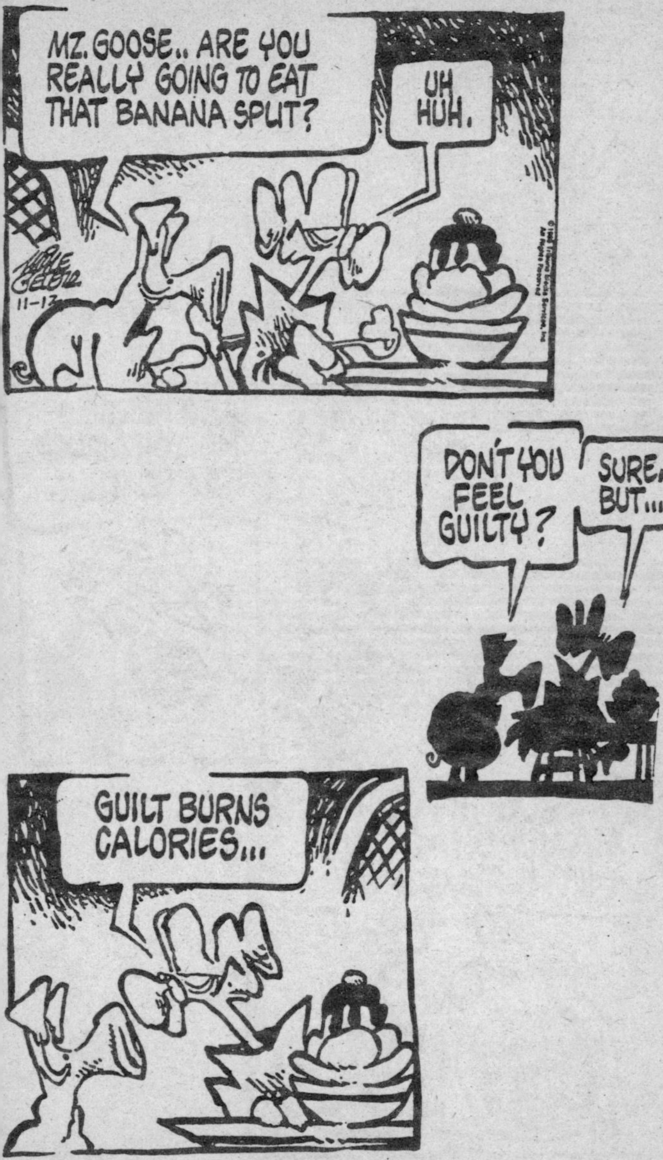
MZ. GOOSE.. ARE YOU REALLY GOING TO EAT THAT BANANA SPLIT?
UH HUH.
DON'T YOU FEEL GUILTY?
SURE, BUT...
GUILT BURNS CALORIES...

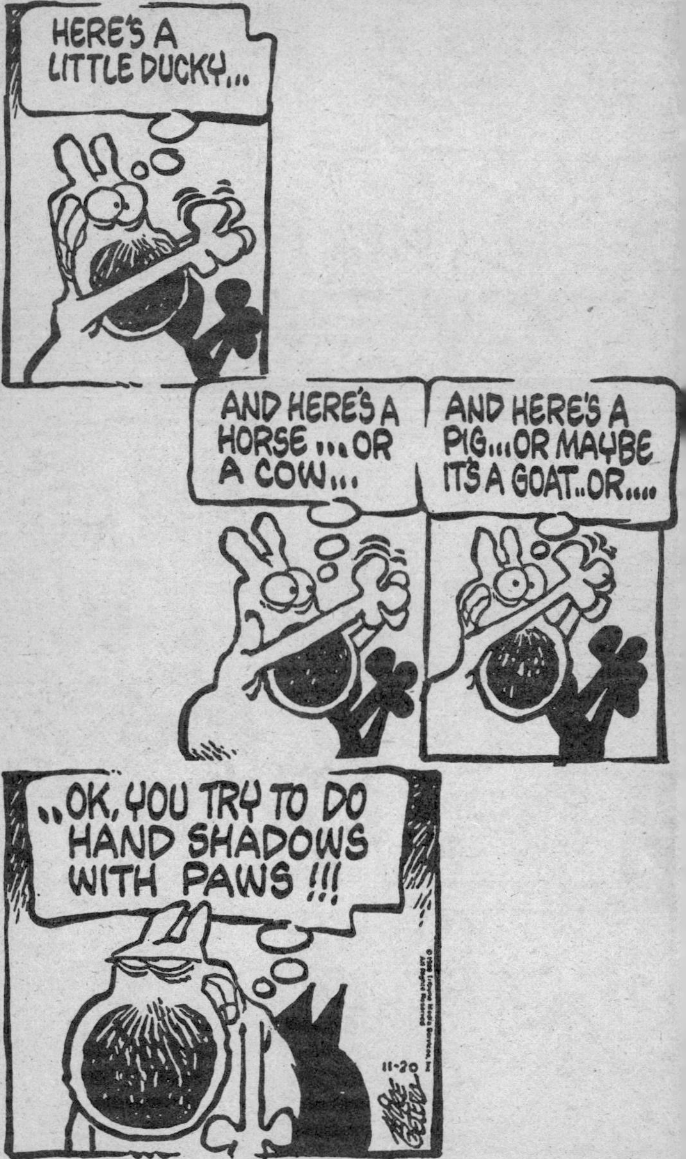
HERE'S A LITTLE DUCKY...
AND HERE'S A HORSE ...OR A COW...
AND HERE'S A PIG....OR MAYBE IT'S A GOAT..OR....
..OK, YOU TRY TO DO HAND SHADOWS WITH PAWS !!!
11-20

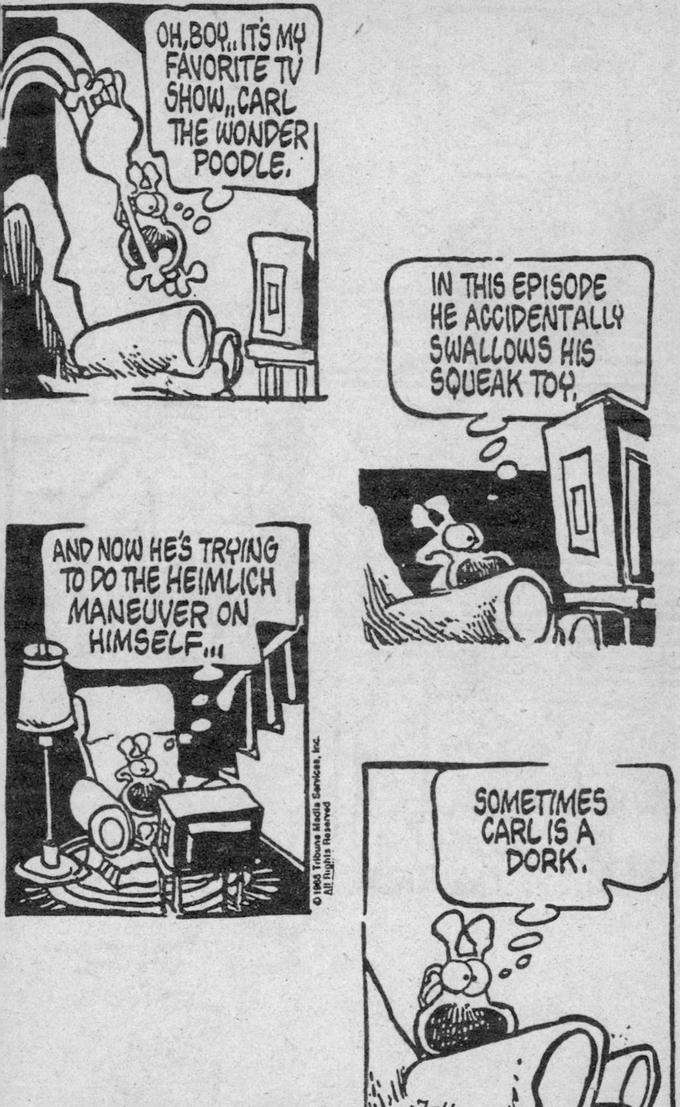
OH, BOY... IT'S MY FAVORITE TV SHOW... CARL THE WONDER POODLE.
IN THIS EPISODE HE ACCIDENTALLY SWALLOWS HIS SQUEAK TOY.
AND NOW HE'S TRYING TO DO THE HEIMLICH MANEUVER ON HIMSELF...
SOMETIMES CARL IS A DORK.
7-11

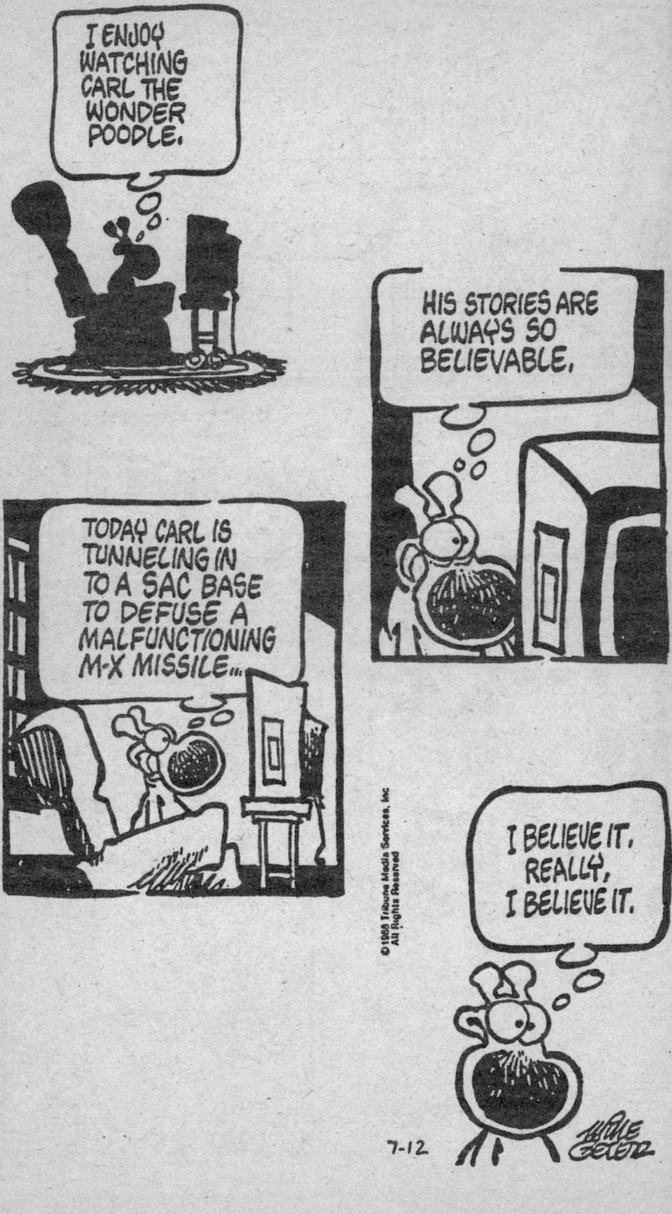
I ENJOY WATCHING CARL THE WONDER POODLE.
HIS STORIES ARE ALWAYS SO BELIEVABLE.
TODAY CARL IS TUNNELING IN TO A SAC BASE TO DEFUSE A MALFUNCTIONING M-X MISSILE...
I BELIEVE IT. REALLY, I BELIEVE IT.
7-12

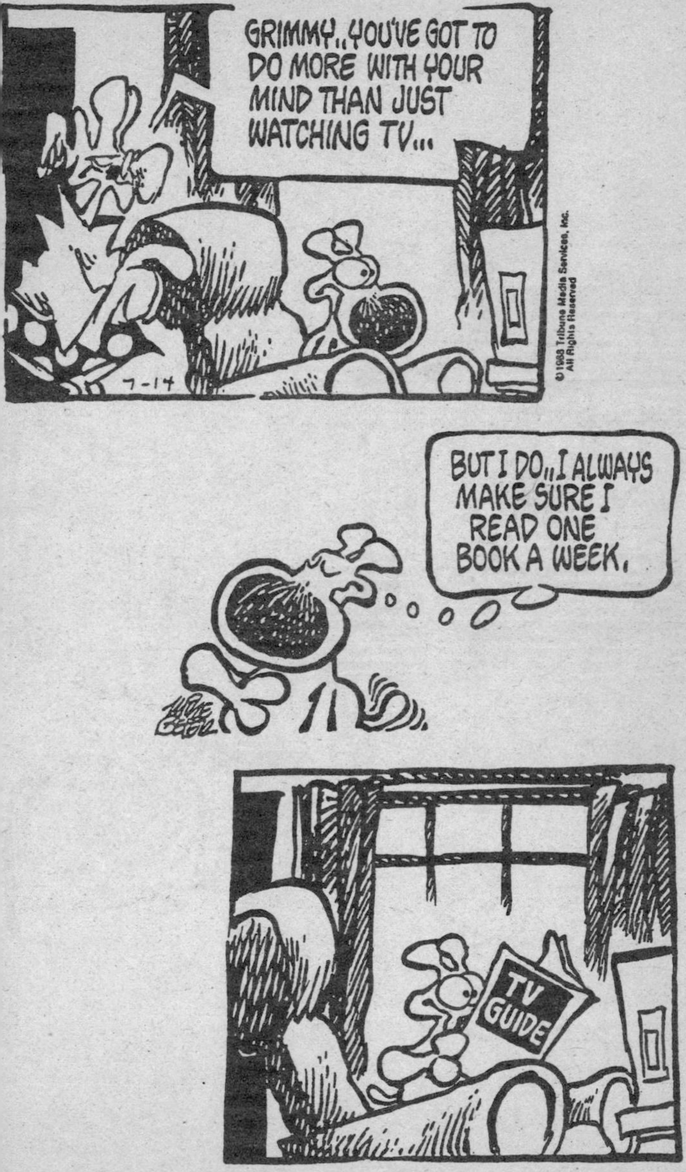
GRIMMY.. YOU'VE GOT TO DO MORE WITH YOUR MIND THAN JUST WATCHING TV...
7-14
© 1988 Tribune Media Services, Inc. All Rights Reserved
BUT I DO.. I ALWAYS MAKE SURE I READ ONE BOOK A WEEK.
TV GUIDE

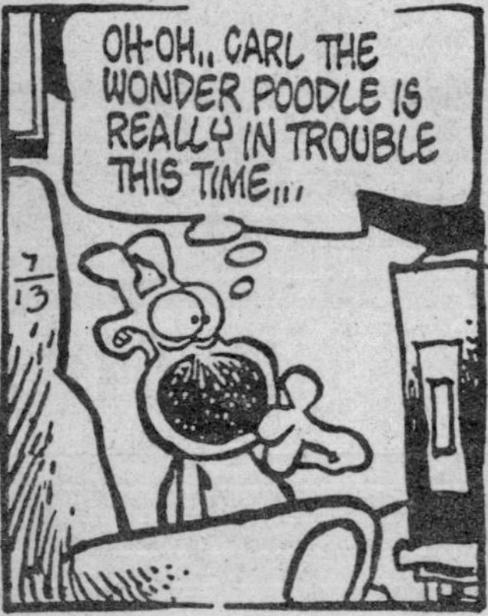
OH-OH,, CARL THE WONDER POODLE IS REALLY IN TROUBLE THIS TIME,,,
7/13

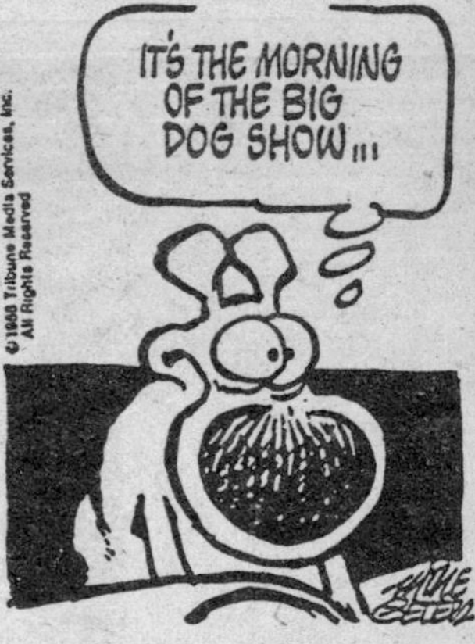
IT'S THE MORNING OF THE BIG DOG SHOW,,,

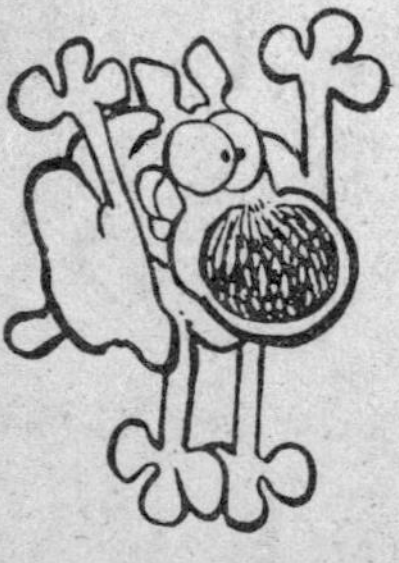

AND ONE OF THE RHINESTONES FELL OUT OF HIS STERLING SILVER DOGGIE COLLAR.

COULDN'T YOU JUST DIE?

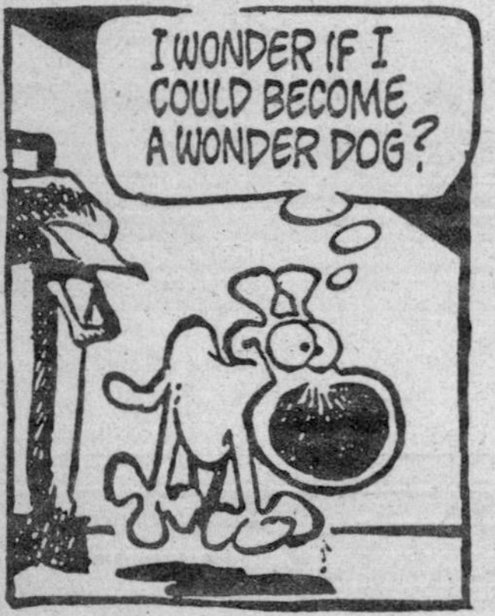
I WONDER IF I COULD BECOME A WONDER DOG?

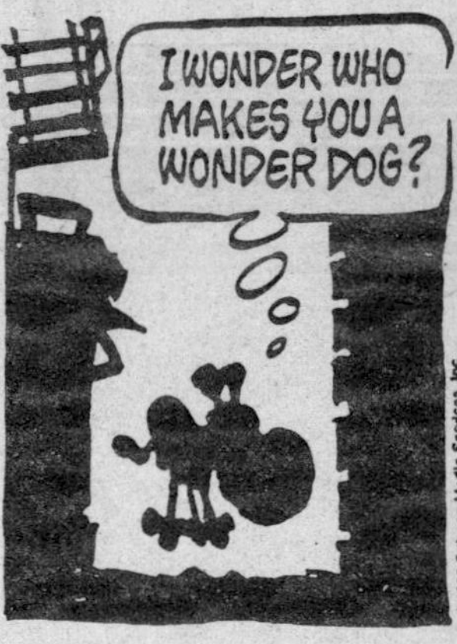
I WONDER WHO MAKES YOU A WONDER DOG?

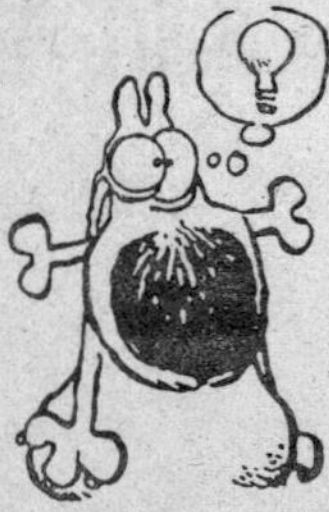

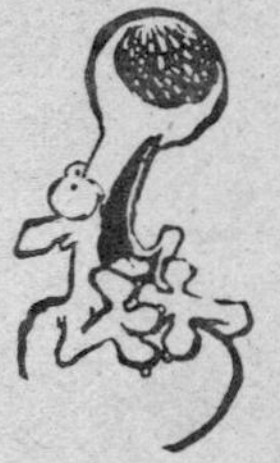

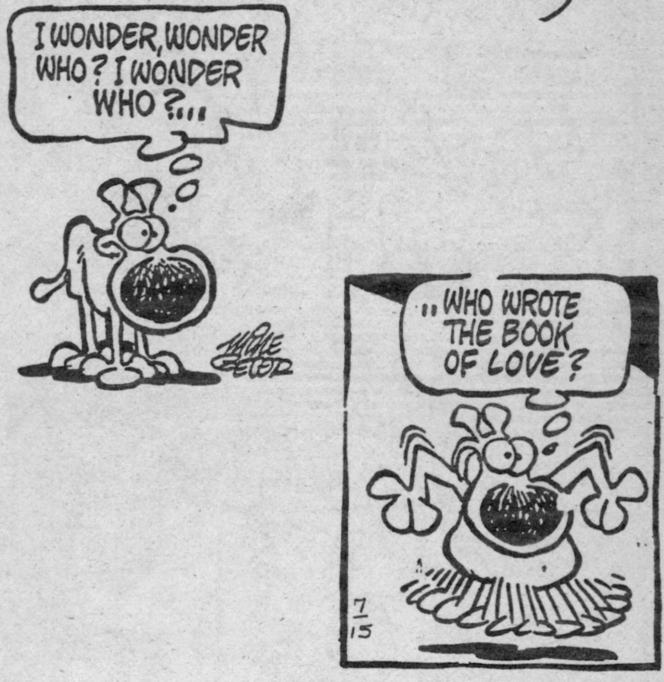

I WONDER, WONDER WHO? I WONDER WHO?...
..WHO WROTE THE BOOK OF LOVE?
7/15

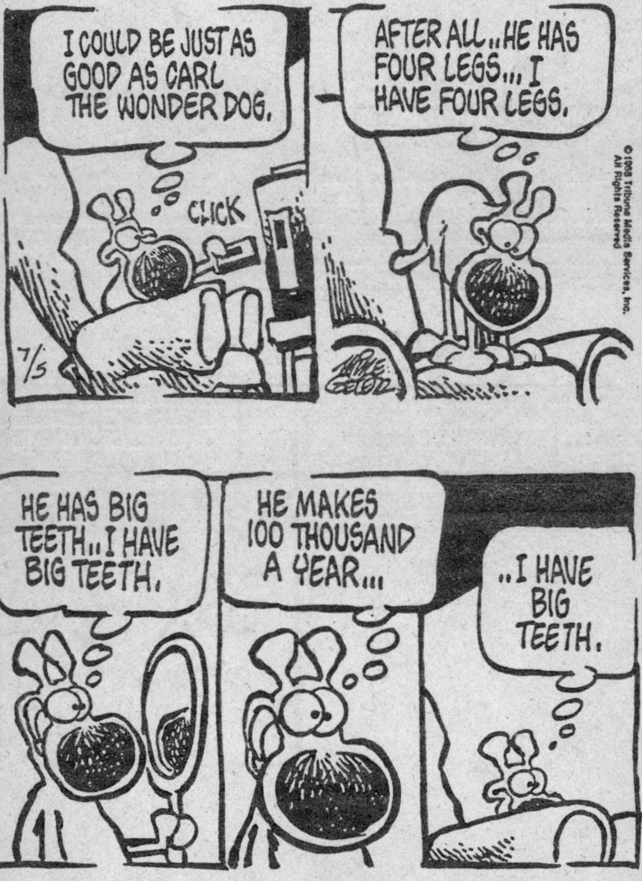
I COULD BE JUST AS GOOD AS CARL THE WONDER DOG.
CLICK
7/5
AFTER ALL.. HE HAS FOUR LEGS.,, I HAVE FOUR LEGS.
HE HAS BIG TEETH.. I HAVE BIG TEETH.
HE MAKES 100 THOUSAND A YEAR...
..I HAVE BIG TEETH.

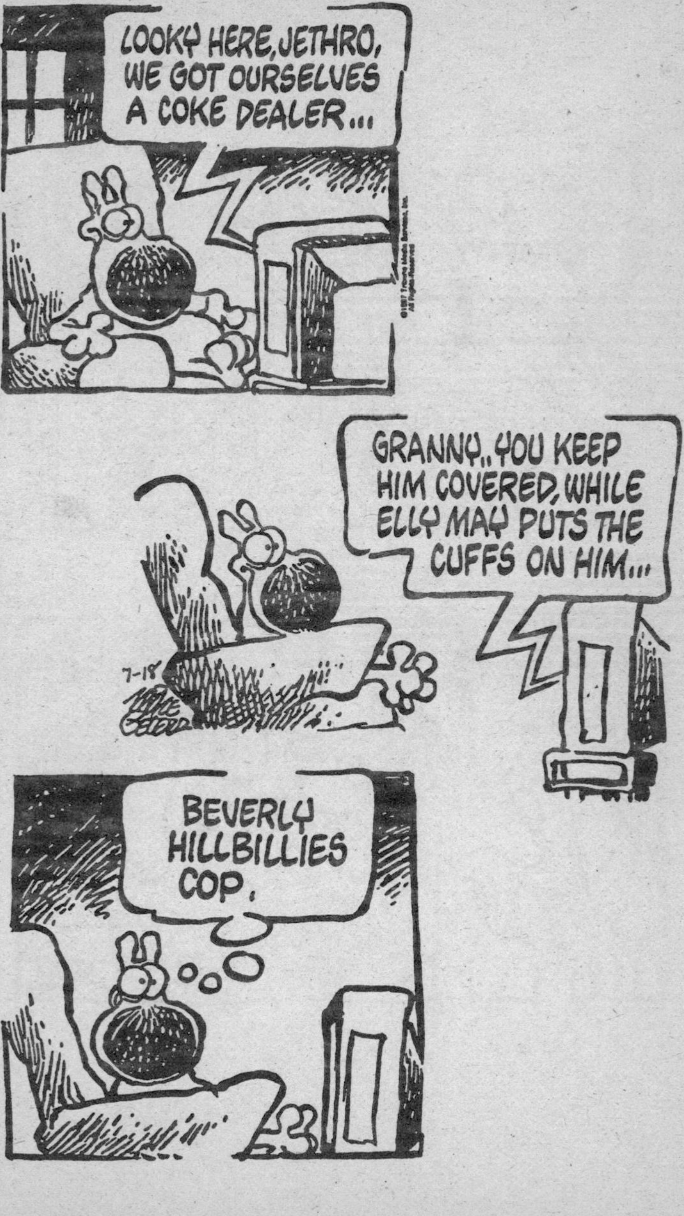
LOOKY HERE, JETHRO, WE GOT OURSELVES A COKE DEALER...
GRANNY.. YOU KEEP HIM COVERED, WHILE ELLY MAY PUTS THE CUFFS ON HIM...
7-18
BEVERLY HILLBILLIES COP.

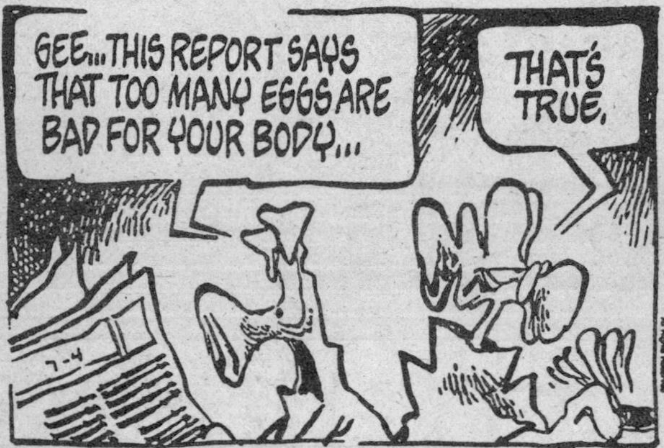
GEE...THIS REPORT SAYS THAT TOO MANY EGGS ARE BAD FOR YOUR BODY...
THAT'S TRUE.
7-4

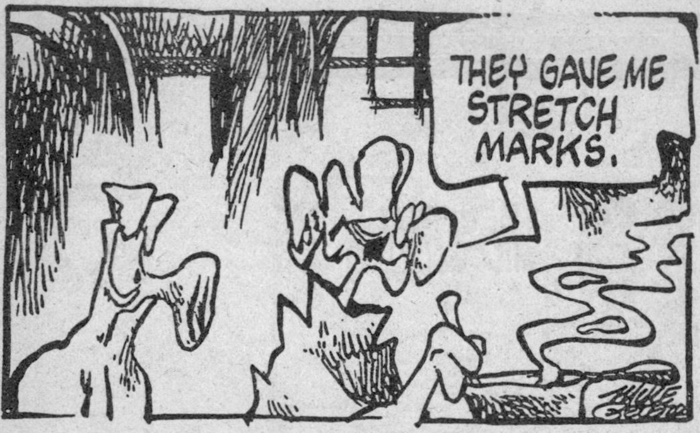
THEY GAVE ME STRETCH MARKS.

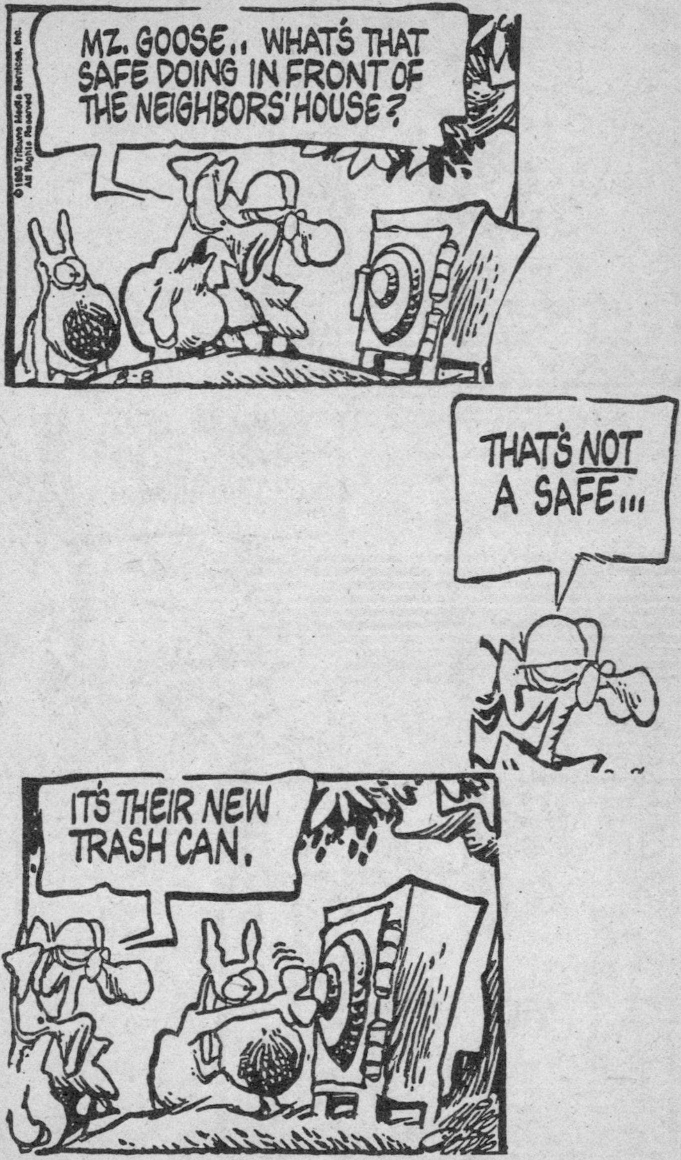
MZ. GOOSE.. WHAT'S THAT SAFE DOING IN FRONT OF THE NEIGHBORS' HOUSE?
THAT'S NOT A SAFE...
IT'S THEIR NEW TRASH CAN.

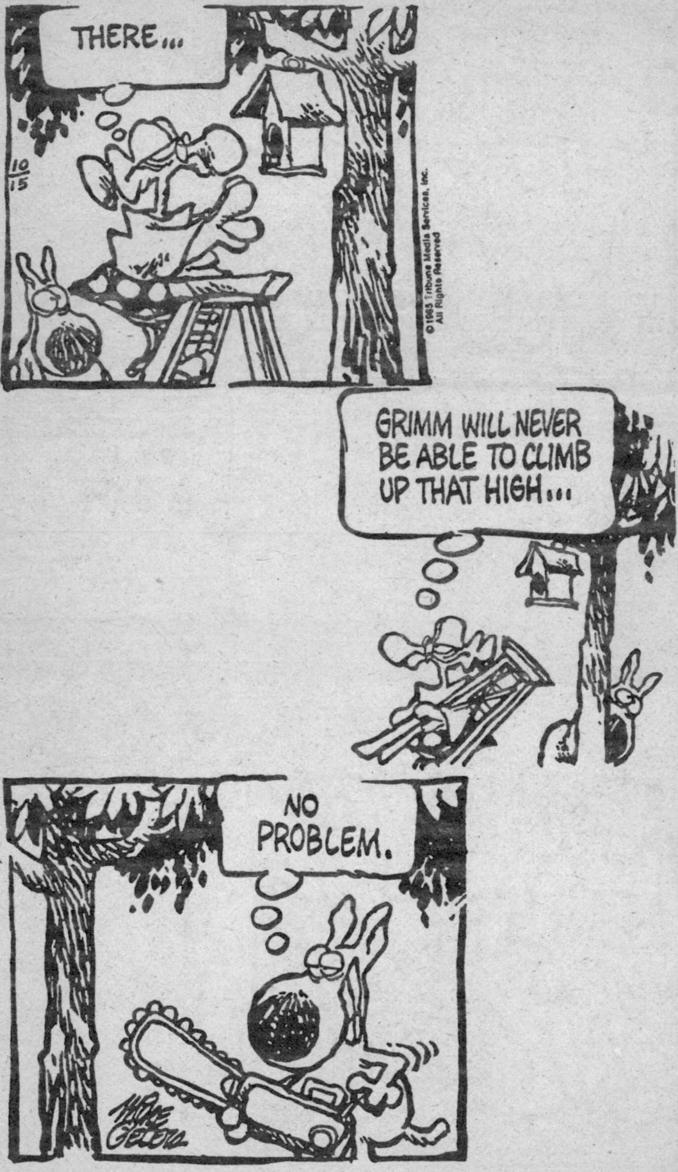
THERE...
10/15
©1985 Tribune Media Services, Inc. All Rights Reserved
GRIMM WILL NEVER BE ABLE TO CLIMB UP THAT HIGH...
NO PROBLEM.

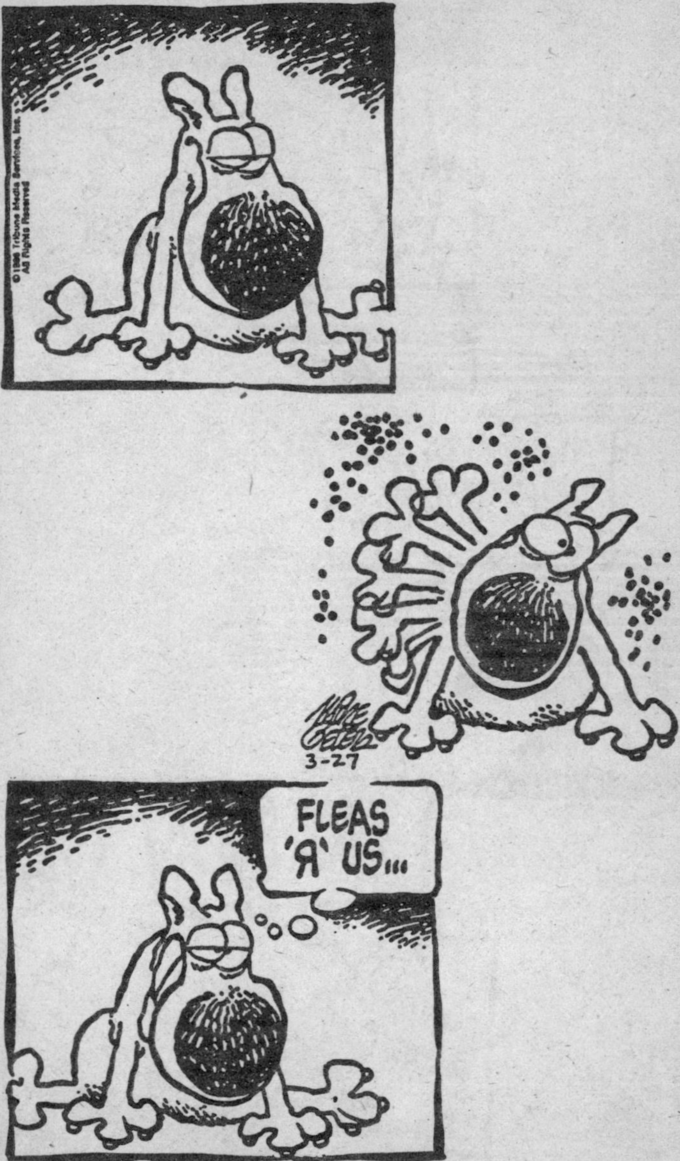
Tribune Media Services, Inc.
All Rights Reserved
3-27
FLEAS 'R' US...

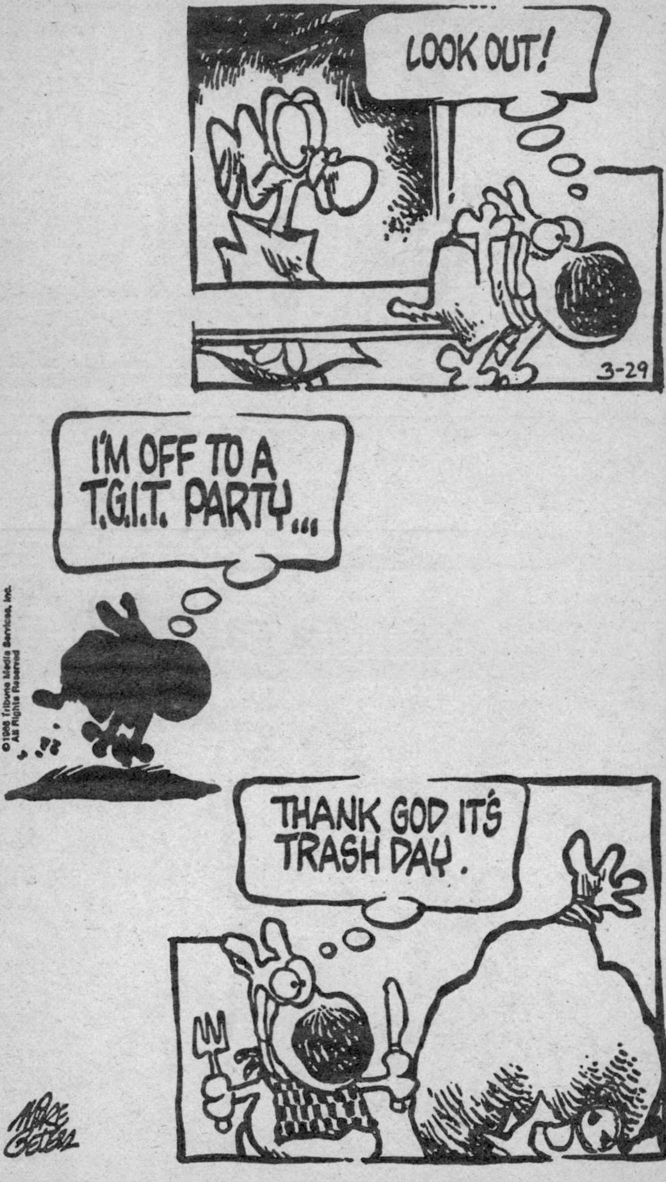
LOOK OUT!
3-29
I'M OFF TO A T.G.I.T. PARTY...
©1986 Tribune Media Services, Inc. All Rights Reserved
THANK GOD IT'S TRASH DAY.

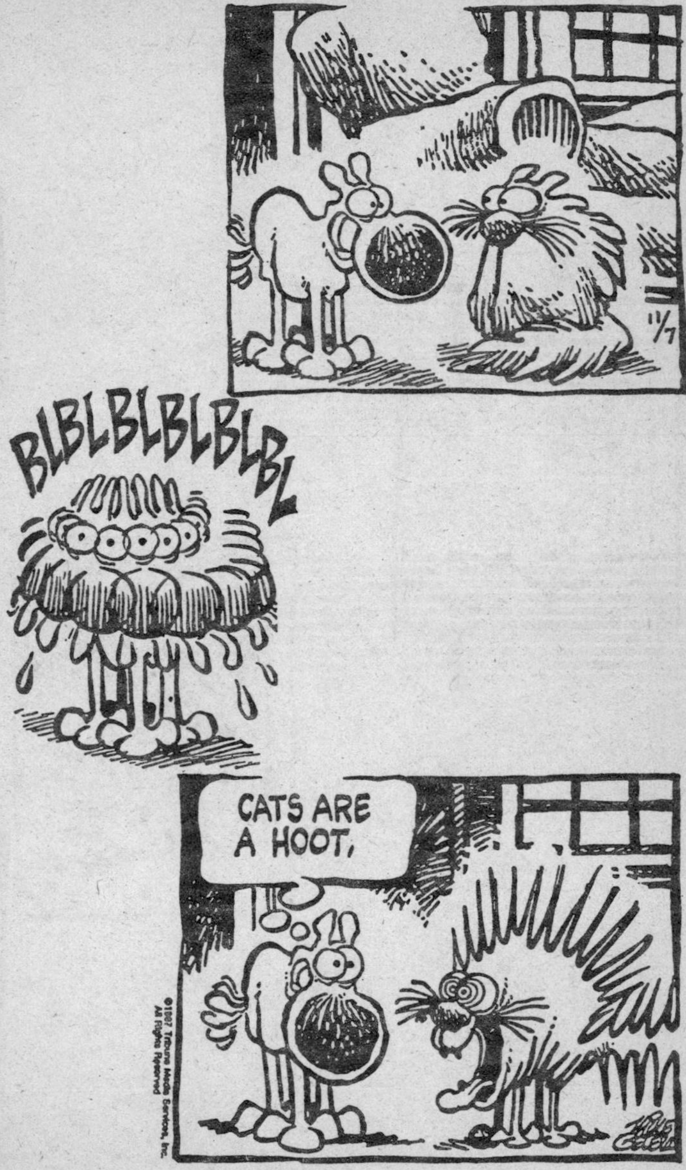

11/7
BLBLBLBLBLBL
CATS ARE A HOOT,
©1987 Tribune Media Services, Inc. All Rights Reserved

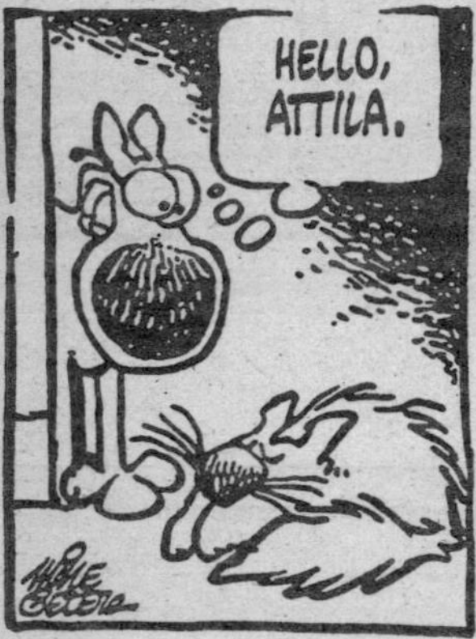
HELLO, ATTILA.

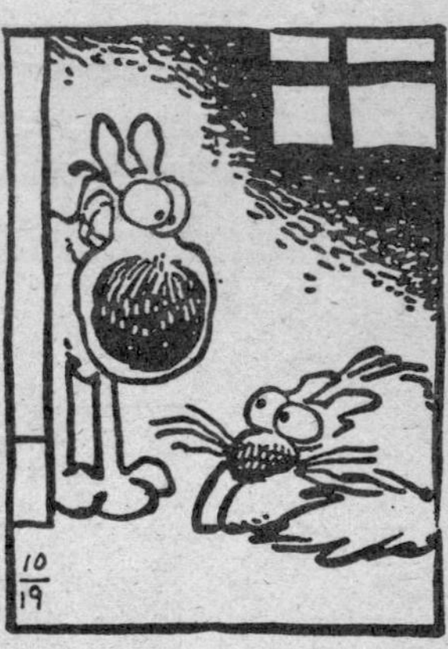
10/19

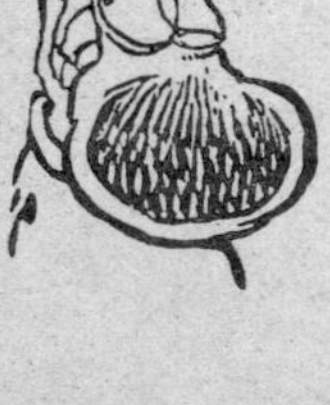

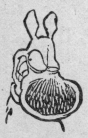

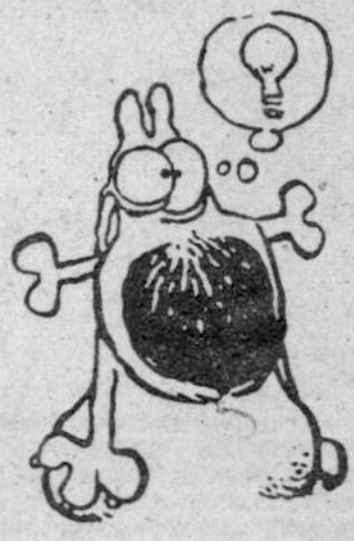

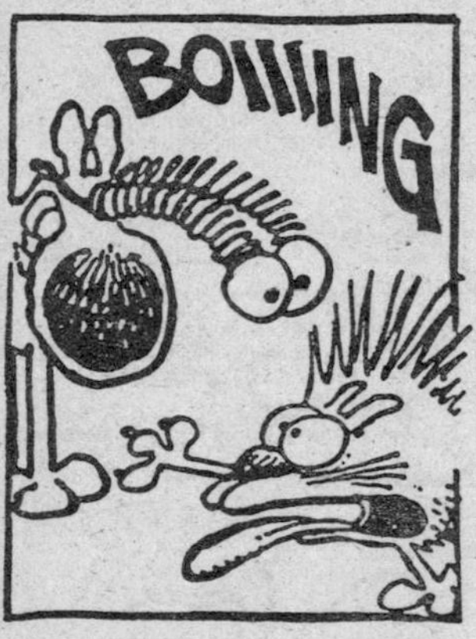
BOIIIING

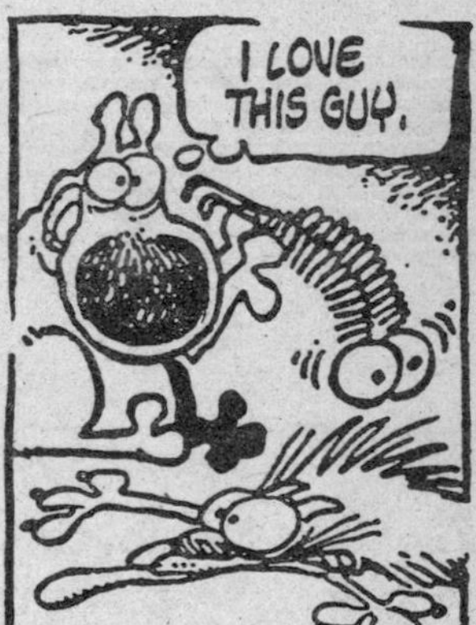
I LOVE THIS GUY.

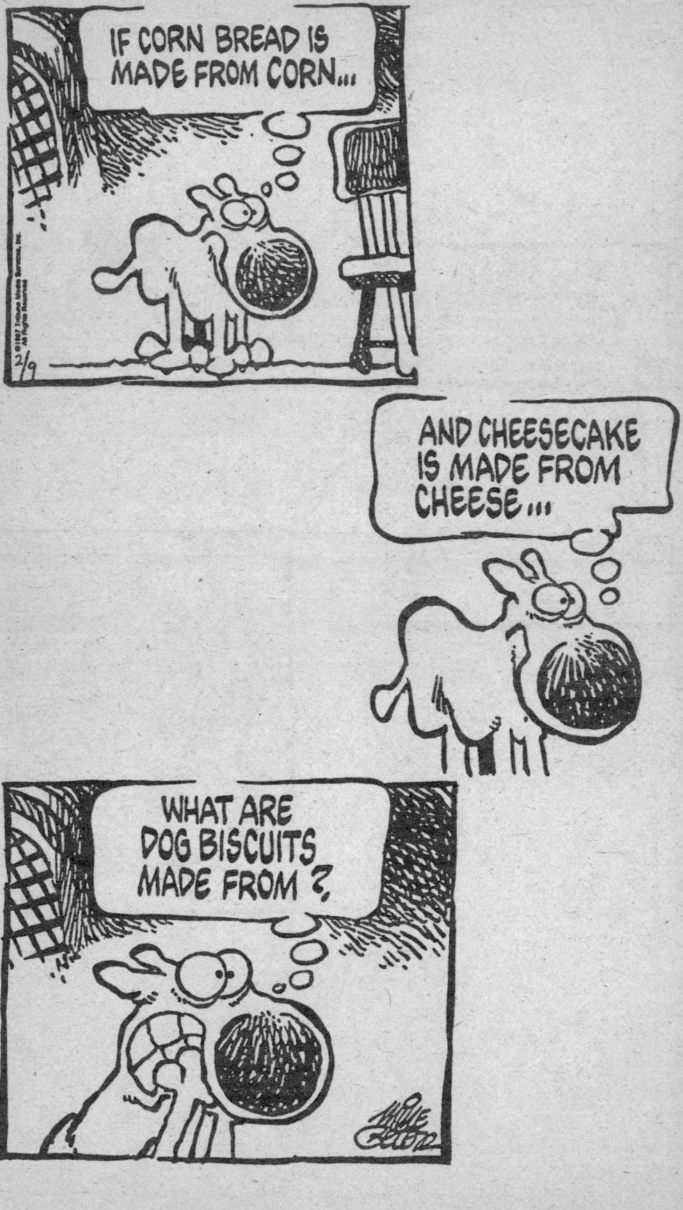
IF CORN BREAD IS MADE FROM CORN...
AND CHEESECAKE IS MADE FROM CHEESE...
WHAT ARE DOG BISCUITS MADE FROM ?

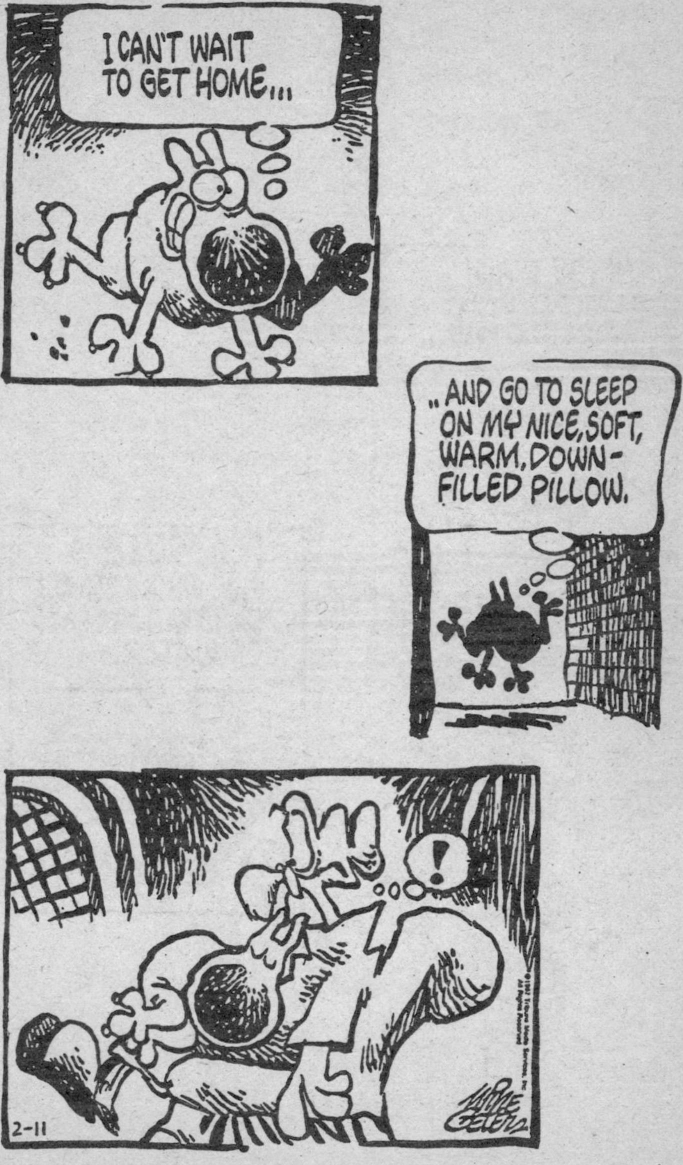
I CAN'T WAIT TO GET HOME...
..AND GO TO SLEEP ON MY NICE, SOFT, WARM, DOWN-FILLED PILLOW.
!
2-11

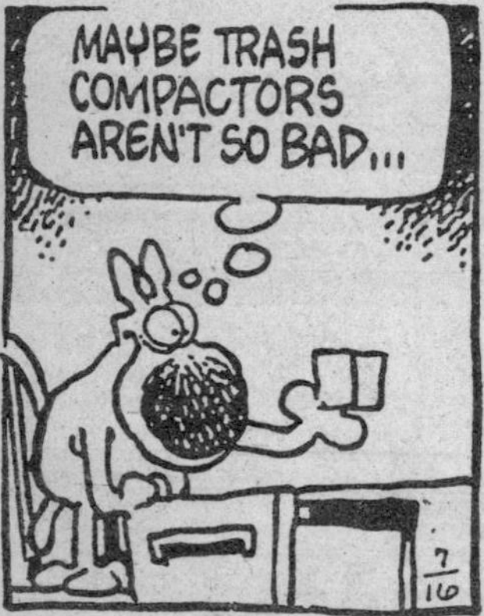
MAYBE TRASH COMPACTORS AREN'T SO BAD...
7/16

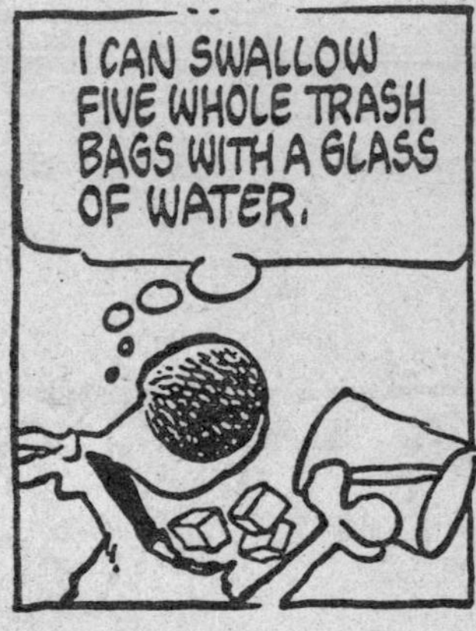
I CAN SWALLOW FIVE WHOLE TRASH BAGS WITH A GLASS OF WATER.

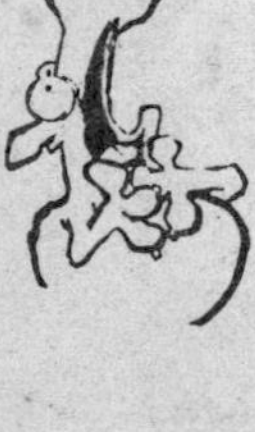

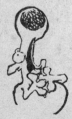

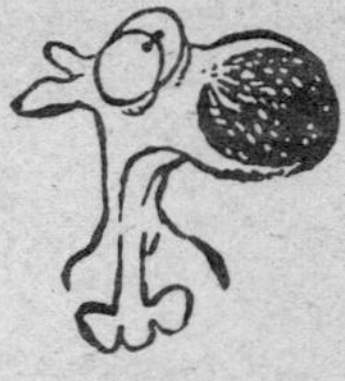

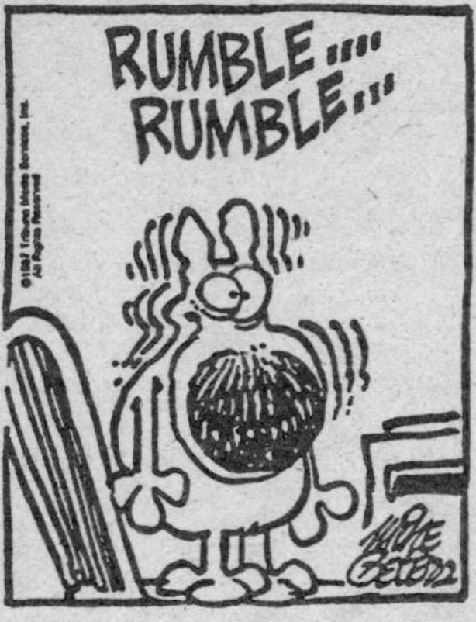
RUMBLE....
RUMBLE...

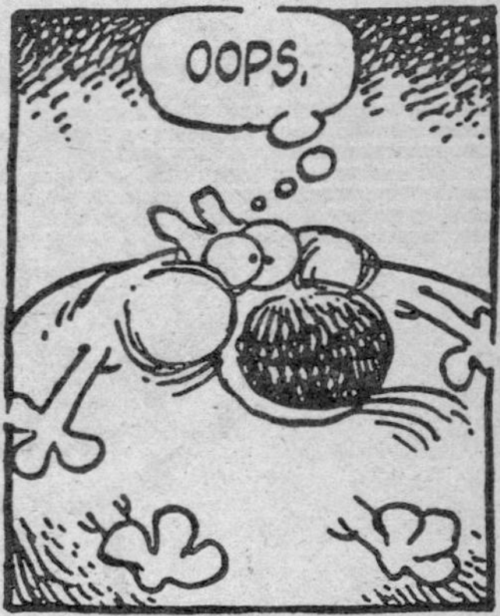
OOPS.

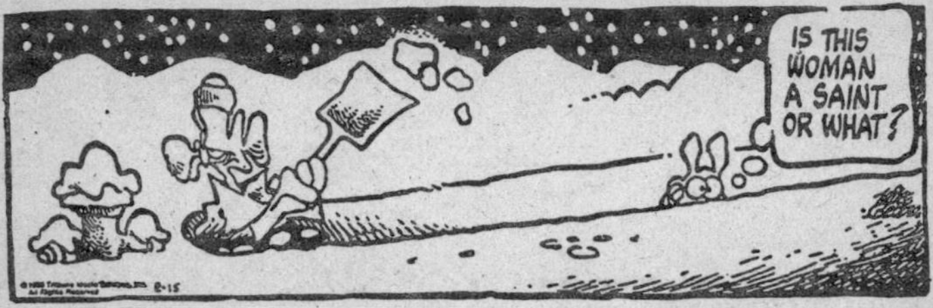
IS THIS WOMAN A SAINT OR WHAT?

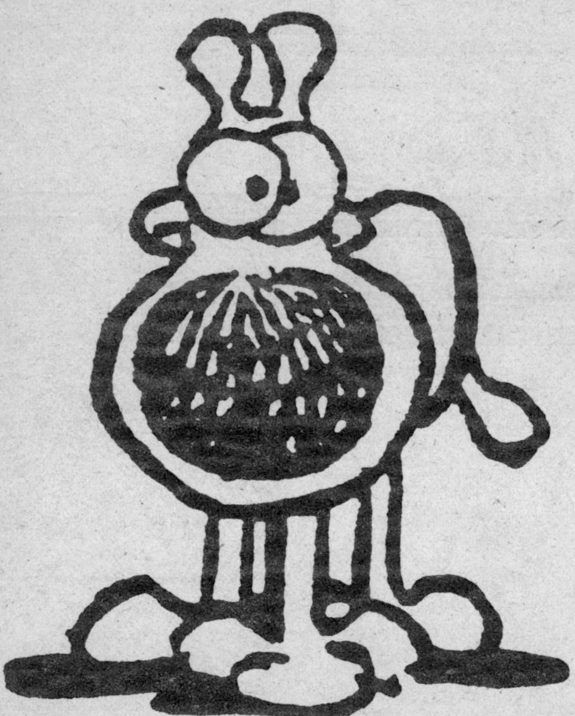

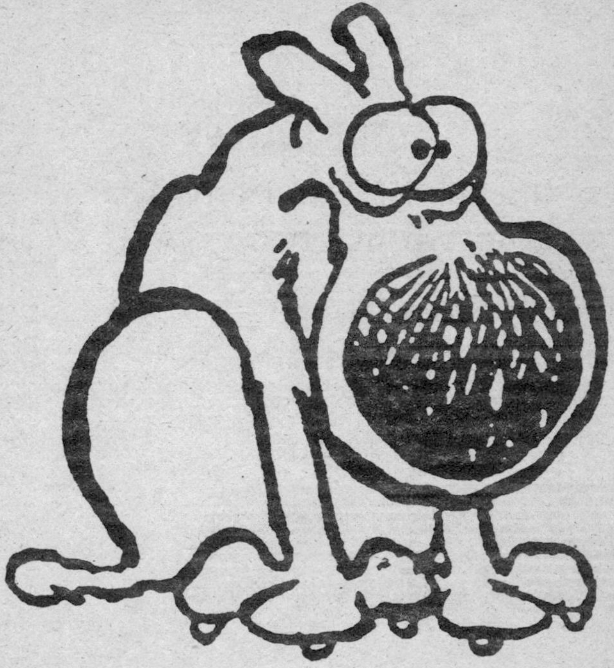

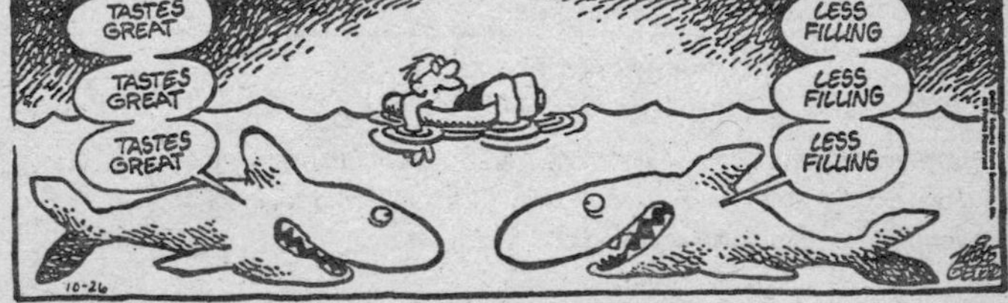
TASTES GREAT
LESS FILLING
TASTES GREAT
LESS FILLING
TASTES GREAT
LESS FILLING
10-26

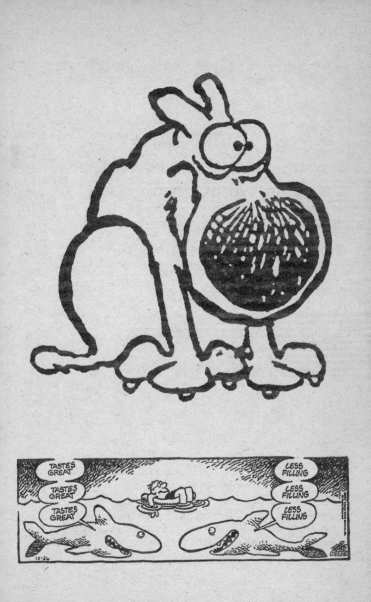

BEETLE BAILEY

THE WACKIEST G.I. IN THE ARMY

☐	56126-0	BEETLE BAILEY: WELCOME TO CAMP SWAMPY!	$3.95
☐	56127-9		Canada $4.95
☐	56109-0	BEETLE BAILEY: THIN AIR	$2.95
☐	56111-2	BEETLE BAILEY: THREE'S A CROWD	$2.95
☐	56068-X	BEETLE BAILEY #4: NOT REVERSE	$1.95
☐	56128-7	BEETLE BAILEY: SEPARATE CHECKS	$3.95
☐	56129-5		Canada $4.95
☐	56092-2	BEETLE BAILEY #8: SURPRISE PACKAGE	$2.50
☐	56093-0		Canada $2.95
☐	56124-4	BEETLE BAILEY: THAT SINKING FEELING	$1.95
☐	56125-2		Canada $2.50

Buy them at your local bookstore or use this handy coupon:
Clip and mail this page with your order.

Publishers Book and Audio Mailing Service
P.O. Box 120159, Staten Island, NY 10312-0004

Please send me the book(s) I have checked above. I am enclosing $_____
(please add $1.25 for the first book, and $.25 for each additional book to
cover postage and handling. Send check or money order only—no CODs.)

Name _____

Address _____

City _____ State/Zip _____

Please allow six weeks for delivery. Prices subject to change without notice.

HAGAR THE HORRIBLE

Buy them at your local bookstore or use this handy coupon:
Clip and mail this page with your order.

Publishers Book and Audio Mailing Service
P.O. Box 120159, Staten Island, NY 10312-0004

Please send me the book(s) I have checked above. I am enclosing $_____
(please add $1.25 for the first book, and $.25 for each additional book to
cover postage and handling. Send check or money order only—no CODs.)

Name _____

Address _____

City _____ State/Zip _____

Please allow six weeks for delivery. Prices subject to change without notice.

HEATHCLIFF

AMERICA'S CRAZIEST CAT

- ☐ 56816-8 HEATHCLIFF: SPECIALTIES ON THE HOUSE $2.50
  56817-X Canada $3.50

- ☐ 56818-4 HEATHCLIFF AT HOME $2.50
  56811-7 Canada $3.50

- ☐ 56819-2 HEATHCLIFF AND THE GOOD LIFE $2.50
  56820-6 Canada $3.50

- ☐ 56814-1 HEATHCLIFF: YOU'RE OUT $2.50
  56815-X Canada $3.50

- ☐ 50633-2 HEATHCLIFF: BEST OF FRIENDS $2.95
  50634-0 Canada $3.95